Say It Right
the First Time

To MYRNA,
A dYNamic
vivacious Communicator.

BEST wishes!

10-3

Say It Right
the First Time

Loretta Malandro, Ph.D.

McGraw-Hill
New York Chicago San Francisco Lisbon London
Madrid Mexico City Milan New Delhi San Juan Seoul
Singapore Sydney Toronto

1 2 3 4 5 6 7 8 9 0 DOC/DOC 0 9 8 7 6 5 4 3

ISBN 0-07-140861-4

McGraw-Hill books are available at special quantity discounts to use as premiums and sales promotions, or for use in corporate training programs. For more information, please write to the Director of Special Sales, Professional Publishing, McGraw-Hill, Two Penn Plaza, New York, NY 10121-2298. Or contact your local bookstore.

 This book is printed on recycled, acid-free paper containing a minimum of 50% recycled, de-inked fiber.

Library of Congress Cataloging-in-Publication Data

Malandro, Loretta A.
    Say it right the first time / by Loretta Malandro.
        p. cm.
Includes index.
    ISBN 0-07-140861-4 (alk. paper)
    1. Interpersonal communication.   2. Oral communication.   I. Title.
HM1166.M35 2003
302—dc21

                                                            2002156361

This book is dedicated to the memory of my mother, Josephine, whose kindness and passion for life inspire me daily, and to my father, Rudy, whose guidance, love, and support are my foundation.

Contents

Acknowledgments

Nothing is ever created by a single person. The people who surround us make all things possible. Inspiration to write this book came from a small, select team who talk straight and hold me accountable for excellence, especially when I become resigned. My father, Rudy, and sister, Rosemary, both financial experts and CPAs, provided logic, reason, and support for why I should write another book. My treasured book coach and friend, Sharon Ellis, encouraged me when I doubted I had enough to say and laughed good-naturedly when I discovered I had too much to say. Judy Lacey, my one-of-a-kind assistant, did the impossible by making sure everything ran smoothly in my life. Sue Cahoon, a constant idea-generator, made sure I used technology appropriately and taught me how to "cut and paste," both literally and metaphorically. Valerie Demetros worked closely with me to make sure we used the right words to talk about using the right words. Nicole Lacey worked hard to make the book "look good" on paper. And Jon Harlow kept me at the top of my game with his encouragement and optimism.

Through the years there have been extraordinary CEOs and corporate leaders who have made a significant difference in my life and have contributed to the messages in this book. A special thanks goes to Gian Fulgoni, Hal Logan, Frank Patalano, Nido Qubein, John Talucci, John Van Brunt, and John Willson. From my roots in the academic world, Dr. Larry Barker and Dr. Kevin Toomb, mentors and dear friends, have encouraged and applauded the use of my creative side.

In each of our lives there is a group of "silent partners," people who are not center stage but who quietly change our lives by their presence. My life choices have been shaped by Chip Dashiell and Susan Maxwell through their expertise, caring, and coaching. Finally, there is my wise editor, Barry Neville, who started me down this path to "write the book that needs to be written." And that's what I've done, with the support of many special people. Thank you all.

Dr. Loretta Malandro

Introduction

There are many different ways to produce high-performance results in organizations. Some companies create an internally competitive environment where the toughest, but not necessarily the most competent, rise to the top. Other organizations build a consensus culture where agreement replaces quality by reducing decisions to the lowest common denominator. Organizations of the future, however, are choosing a longer-term approach to producing results by investing in people. The most prized possession in these companies is the high level of *accountability* and *collaboration* among people. People are placed at the heart of the organization, and leaders recognize that their most important resource walks through the front door every day and will walk out again if they are uninspired.

This book is for leaders and managers at all levels who believe that *how people work together* is the key to long-term success. Several premises underlie this belief:

1. People want to do their best.

2. People will give their discretionary effort when they are inspired.

3. People will produce unprecedented results with inspired leadership.

Communication, language in particular, is the vehicle for unleashing the power of people. This is the tool that leaders use to either motivate people to reach higher or to derail them completely. Words are potent. They move the action forward or backward; there is no such thing as a neutral comment from a leader. All words have meaning and impact. Leaders who understand this can use language to harness the boundless energy of people toward focused business outcomes. Those who fail to recognize the power of their words will find themselves frustrated with the constant cycle of rework and communication breakdowns. The truth is that leadership competence, expertise, and commitment will not overcome poor communication skills.

Most competent leaders and managers have been schooled, both formally and informally, in many different facets of leadership. But few have had the opportunity to learn how words shape reality and determine both their future and the future of the organization. This book closes the gap by providing leaders with much more than just tools; it explains *why the tools work* so leaders can easily apply powerful communication principles to the many challenges they face.

Because words are potent, this book does not waste them. It is to the point, practical, and direct. No time is wasted on theory, academic research, or ego massage. This book is specifically designed for leaders and managers who are already successful and who want to achieve much more through their best resource people.

Your Power and How It Impacts People

100% Accountability

Harnessing the Power of Your Words

Your Purpose

To inspire positive action in others by **communicating accountably** at all times.

The meaning of a word is the action it produces.

Ashley Montague

It's 9 a.m. and another day at the office has begun. The conference room is buzzing with activity, the coffee is brewed, and discussions of weekend excursions have subsided. But nervous energy from managers and whispered chatter follow the company's leader as she enters the conference room and takes her seat.

"We've had a terrible fourth quarter," she begins, looking around the room as eyes avoid her. "Revenues are down 11 percent and expenses are up 14 percent. You're supposed to be managing this situation, not sitting around letting everything fall apart. What are we paying you for anyway?"

She pauses and looks around the room. Complete silence. "Starting today, I want all unnecessary spending cut out of your budgets. I want immediate increased productivity from your people, and I don't care how you get it—just get it!"

The message is clear, direct, and completely demoralizing. While barking out orders and expressing her frustration, the leader has managed to alienate her managers in less than 30 seconds. Her words are unharnessed energy, producing chaos, anxiety, and uncertainty. She is unaware of anything but her immediate personal mission—get this situation corrected fast. The only way to do this, she reasons, is to get her people in high gear.

Unfortunately, the leader has produced disastrous results. Her people are in high gear all right—they are stressed and frenzied. No one is thinking; everyone is reacting. The problems do not stop here. Her emotionally charged words will be branded in the minds of everyone who attended the meeting. But the leader's words are not contained; the managers repeat them to whomever will listen. This unharnessed energy erupts into an organizational wildfire, leaving people in a paralyzed state. Morale is nonexistent, decisions are poor or not made at all, and productivity is at an all-time low.

Words can either get you in trouble by derailing and frustrating others, or they can be used as a powerful vehicle to inspire people to excel. Over the past 20 years I have worked with CEOs and leaders at all levels who are baffled as to why their words create problems or, at bare minimum, do not produce the results they want. They are surprised when people react, annoyed when they do not act, and disappointed when their words are misunderstood. Most leaders operate under the illusion that what they say is what people hear. This is simply not true. Communication is much more involved, and once you add the dimension of power and authority, the problem compounds. Leaders must work through an intricate maze of how others filter, interpret, and add personal meaning to their messages. Although communication is complex, it can be easy. This may sound contradictory, but it is not. Superstitions, myths, and beliefs about how people *should* respond and behave add the dimension of complexity to communication. If leaders could lead without illusions or unrealistic expectations, disappointment would disappear and superior work would be accomplished.

It's time to bring back the fundamental and enduring communication principles guaranteed to make everyone's life easier. This book provides clear-cut guidelines that will eliminate unnecessary frustration and time by dramatically increasing your ability to say it right the first time and recover quickly when you don't. Harnessing the power of words and effortlessly producing the impact you want makes being a leader fun, enriching, and rewarding. If it's not, what's the point? Money, enticing financial packages, and other perks only help you endure what you do not like. Managers and leaders need to be inspired and have the courage to be different. It doesn't matter if you are an informal leader without a title or a top-level executive. You may be the owner of a small business, a supervisor, a mid-level manager, a partner in a law firm, or the CEO of a large organization. The only thing that matters is that you enjoy making the impossible happen by mobilizing people and helping them do things they never thought they could. If making a difference through people energizes and lights a fire inside you, you are reading the right book.

The purpose of this chapter is to begin the process of uncovering the key, underlying communication principles that have made good leaders great. All you have to do is sit back, relax, and set your beliefs aside. This is the most difficult request I will make of you. I am asking you to start with a clean slate by suspending your opinion about how people should or should not react when you communicate. If you accept this request and are willing to examine your communication behavior as a leader, then we can begin the journey together.

Delusions of Adequacy

With the rapid pace of change, you barely have enough time to handle pressing business issues, let alone think about word choice and selection. But you'll pay the price for this oversight. Perhaps you're like many other leaders who do not recognize the impact their words have on others until it is too late. One day something happens, and your hot buttons are pushed. The buzz saw starts up, and your words just spill out. People react, and you react to their reaction. Now you have a problem. You will spend considerable time and energy cleaning up the damage created by poorly chosen words that have unconsciously escaped from your lips.

Perhaps you have a different challenge. You seldom react and attack people with words, but you don't inspire them either. People listen to what you have to say, but they are not fired up and ready to make the impossible happen. They respond in what appears to be a normal and receptive manner, except they are not giving you their extra energy and effort. Why should they? Your words are not compelling.

You may find yourself disappointed by the performance of others. You deliver clear, straightforward expectations and rightfully expect others to execute them effectively. But wait a minute—just because you think your expectations are clear does not mean others do. If you find yourself disappointed by a gap in what you expect and what people deliver, your words may be the culprit.

> **This book is not about being perfect.**
> *It is about saying it right the first time and recovering quickly when you don't.*

In spite of its importance, most leaders seldom think about what they say. It is like breathing—something that requires little conscious effort. Words come out of your mouth, form sentences, and result in what is referred to as "communication." Answer this question: "Do you consider yourself to be a good communicator?" Let's presume you answer affirmatively and vigorously avow you are not only a good communicator but also an inspirational one. This may be the problem. *Your* opinion is not relevant. How you think you communicate and affect others is immaterial; it's what others think that matters. The probability is high that you have delusions of adequacy about your ability to communicate as a leader. But let's not trust my opinion either. How others respond to you is the only accurate measure of your effectiveness. If you unintentionally evoke negative reactions, or you repeat the same message over and over again and listeners still don't get it, or morale is not at the expected level, the problem may be what is coming out of your mouth, not what is wrong with their ears.

What you need is a way to replace ineffective, automatic, and habitual word patterns with good word choices. Here's the catch—

just because you talk to people on a daily basis does not mean you do it well. You may think that talking—selecting the appropriate words and having conversations with others—is a skill you have already mastered. If you have this belief, you will have to suspend it in order to learn something new. The trap that leaders fall into over and over again is thinking they already have the answers. What you think you know can get you in trouble in all walks of life, and it is the greatest barrier to becoming an extraordinary leader.

Leaders must have the courage to learn, make mistakes, and be flat out wrong. It is easier to let go of delusions of adequacy when you recognize that leaders everywhere, whether at the top or bottom tiers of an organization, are all the same—fallible human beings who slip up and blunder. Somewhere along the way leaders started to believe they had to be right and that people expected them to have all the answers. Organizations hired them to plot the accurate direction and make the correct decisions. But when leaders and managers try to live up to expectations of being right all the time, it creates big problems for them and those who must live and work with them. It is best to remember the principle used in systems thinking: "The most powerful system (or person) is the most flexible one." If you are willing to give up being right and come face-to-face with the reality of not having all the answers, you are on your way to building a quality that only extraordinary leaders have—tremendous flexibility in how they think, behave, and speak.

A Leader's Choice: 50/50 or 100% Accountability

You have a choice—to allow your words to run amuck and deal with the damage and fallout as it occurs, or harness their power to inspire people to produce consistent, outstanding results. With every choice there are payoffs and consequences. Leaving words unharnessed means you could save time on the front end. This sounds like a payoff since you would not need to spend time crafting your messages. Nor would you need to take accountability for how your words affect others. It simply would not matter. When a problem occurs, such as low morale, an organizational reaction, or a significant drop in performance, you'll deal with it. The consequences, however, are huge: You will spend at least 10 times the effort trying to recover from communication breakdowns than you would in preventing them. In the process you'll lose talented people who will leave the company either physically or emotionally, your credibility will erode, and morale will slide dangerously downhill.

If you choose to harness the power of your words and accept accountability for how they impact others, you will have different payoffs and consequences. You will have to spend time up front to prevent communication breakdowns. You will think about words and how people hear them. Words, and their power, will take on new meaning for you. Yes, you will spend more time on the front end, but you will considerably reduce the time you spend repairing damage. After reading this book, you will have an arsenal of weapons to fight the wars of ambiguity, chaos, uncertainty, anxiety, confusion, low morale, and poor performance. If you use this book as your leader's guide on communication, you will develop powerful skills, learn unbeatable strategies, and master key principles that will guide you daily in making good word choices and decisions.

The crux of your choice lies in whether you are willing to be 100% accountable for your impact on people and create an environment where others do the same. The word *accountability* is often used when describing a 50/50 relationship where people do their share and expect others to carry their own load. It sounds reasonable, but as a business practice it does not work. The 50/50 approach is conditional and depends on what other people do. What happens when others do not do their part or take responsibility for results? Using the 50/50 model, the action stops, fingers are pointed, and a stalemate occurs. The conditional nature of the model is revealed with the implied "if"—"I will do my job *if* you do yours"—a condition that can derail even the best performers and leaders. When this condition is not met, people become resigned and disappointed. Waiting, expecting, or hoping that others will take action is a powerless feeling that others do not enjoy. People want to feel powerful and have a purpose that allows them to grow and stretch. The 50/50 model of accountability is insufficient.

> *Accountable communication is being 100% responsible for how your words impact others.*

The model of 100% accountability is far more powerful for creating feelings of ownership rather than victimization. By accepting 100% accountability, people take responsibility for their impact on business results and each other. No one waits for the goodwill of others to take action. Although it's nice when others step up to the plate, it is not essential for this model to work. Full accountability places the attention on what people can do regardless of what others choose to do. This is the only model that gives you the power to make choices and decisions and design your future the way you want it without waiting for others to do it. It also increases your responsibility for how you affect people. If you choose to be 100% accountable, you can no longer hide behind "They need to listen better." They don't have to listen better; you need to communicate more effectively. The responsibility is on you to alter how people respond to your messages.

> ## 100% ACCOUNTABILITY IS . . .
> - *Choosing to be an OWNER in everything you do.*
> - *Accepting responsibility (not blame) for your impact on results and people.*
> - *Focusing on what you can do instead of waiting for others to act.*

Do not confuse accepting accountability with accepting blame. When people say, "I'm accountable," they often think it means, "I'm to blame." These two concepts are not the same. Being 100% accountable is a personal choice to be an owner and move things forward in spite of challenging people and circumstances. When people act as owners, their focus is on fixing the problem rather than fixing the blame. There are seven keys to accountable communication and every one has an "I" focus. In other words, "I" must learn how to "talk straight responsibly" in order to help others feel that it is safe to speak up and contribute. The ownership, and control, of the response you get rests with you, no one else.

The Seven Keys to Speaking Accountably

1. **Talk straight responsibly.** Being appropriately direct, honest, and straightforward raises trust and credibility. Leaders

who tell the truth fare much better in producing results than those who withhold thoughts and information.

2. **Inspire positive action.** When your attention is on inspiring positive action in others, you will naturally communicate in a more uplifting manner. Even difficult conversations can result in positive outcomes and leave people encouraged to make things happen.

3. **Collaborate with others.** Leaders who place a premium on partnership and collaboration do not tolerate silo behavior, bunker mentality or we/they thinking. These leaders know that working well with others is a necessity for speed and flexibility, a competitive advantage in any market.

4. **Build ownership.** People fall into one of two camps—victims or owners. When challenging circumstances and people appear to control one's life, victim mentality emerges and organizations are fraught with complaints and finger-pointing. Leaders who inspire ownership build an environment in which people are accountable for results *and* their impact on others.

5. **Commit with integrity.** Casual and broken promises are replaced with authentic commitments. The informal use of language is eliminated and in its place is accountable communication where words carry real meaning. People make commitments they plan to keep and responsibly break or renegotiate a promise when necessary.

6. **Hold people accountable.** Leaders who make positive demands on people for quality and excellence get the best results. By holding themselves and others accountable for high

standards, promises, and agreements, leaders raise the bar on both morale and performance.

7. **Recover quickly.** Perfection is not the quest; recovering quickly is the goal. Leaders who acknowledge their mistakes and use breakdowns and problems as learning experiences increase creativity, innovation, and risk-taking. People are more willing to speak up and contribute, making them part of a winning team.

The communication principles, skills, and techniques presented in this book are based on your accepting 100% accountability for your impact on others. If you're not willing to do this, the lessons in this book won't help you. On the other hand, if you are willing to set aside what you think you already know and be responsible for how others respond to what you say, this is exactly the book you want. Not only will you gain powerful skills and insight about how to say it right the first time, you will learn keys to extraordinary leadership that few leaders ever master. Most importantly, your career as a leader will be easier and much more rewarding as you unleash your ability and that of others. Learning how to spot when your communication is off-track is a good starting place. You need finely tuned radar to recognize when it is necessary to correct something you are saying or have already said.

Your Communication Is Off-Track When

- **People are bored and uninterested.** They continue to do what they have always done with no change in their behavior.

- **People are confused and cannot re-create your message.** They have no idea (or many different ideas) about what you said and what you want.

- **People are overwhelmed.** They are paralyzed by too much information coupled with a lack of clarity and direction. They do not act.

- **People are emotionally charged.** People are reacting. You hit a hot button, and they are no longer listening.

To be an outstanding leader or manager who produces high performance, resignation and skepticism must be replaced with accountability and ownership. The quest for 100% accountability is not for leaders who want to be successful: It is for leaders who have already achieved success and want much more. By communicating accountably, you will see instant positive results.

Your Communication Is Accountable When

- **People are inspired.** They go into action to make things happen.

- **People re-create your message for others.** They use their own words to restate what you want and when you want it.

- **People know what is important.** They are clear about your priorities and what needs to happen first.

- **People are emotionally and intellectually engaged.** Your message has tapped both their hearts and minds.

Inspiring Positive Action

Words and conversations fall into two categories: those that move things forward and those that move things backward. Speaking is an action. There is no such thing as neutral or standing still. Technical competence, business expertise, and a strong work ethic will not overcome poor communication skills. Each time a manager speaks one-on-one or to a group, an organizational message is sent. How that message impacts people directly affects morale and performance and can either build or destroy the leader's credibility.

When leaders send messages that are not clear about what they want to say and how they want people to feel, the results are disastrous. How many times have you sent a message, verbal or written, without fully considering the impact it would have on others? Many leaders have fallen from favor because they were not accountable for their words. Once spoken, you cannot erase and record over.

Let's start by taking a look at your day-to-day life. You probably receive more than 100 e-mails per day, 50 voice mails, and a dozen memos. Your life is filled with a constant influx of words and information, and it does not matter whether you are a CEO, supervisor, manager, business owner, or an informal leader.

Does it feel as if you are racing against time when you respond to e-mails, answer voice mails, or engage in a quick, unplanned hallway conversation? You end up managing information that crosses your desk in order to avoid a pileup of demands, problems, and other time-consuming tasks. You may do what many others do—spend your weekends clearing your desk and responding to messages just to avoid starting the week in the hole.

> *Your competence, expertise, and commitment as a leader*
> *will **not** overcome poor communication skills.*
> *Sorry.*

Massive amounts of information and the need for speedy replies are the two greatest enemies in communicating effectively. Everyone is demanding quick decisions and responses from you. In addition, you are constantly putting out unplanned and time-consuming fires. As a result, you probably spend more time reacting than thinking. Communication was easier before there was so much of it. In the morass of paper and technology, we have forgotten the purpose of communication. We used to communicate to connect with people, to create a sense of belonging and community. These are the same reasons why many people prefer working in an organization rather than on their own. Today we mistake information transfer for communication.

When leaders focus on providing information, such as announcing organizational changes, they often fail to consider how people will react. Instinctively you may recognize when dialogue is needed, but in the end a quick memo or e-mail wins out because it's easier and more expedient. The need for speed overrides the precision, quality, and impact of a message. To make matters worse, what you think you are saying is not what listeners hear. Your messages are filtered, interpreted, and reacted to in unpredictable ways.

When leaders focus on inspiring positive action instead of transferring information, they significantly increase morale and dramatically improve performance. The reason for this is straightforward—when the focus is on what people experience and feel, then how you communicate and how others respond drastically changes. The only way to harness the power of words is to treat speaking as an action.

In the land of 100% accountability, you have a specific purpose to fulfill each time you communicate. Your job is to inspire positive action and bring out the best in people. This includes changing how they think, inspiring them about possibilities they cannot see, and helping others move beyond areas in which they are stuck or resigned. It also means getting people to collaborate, move with urgency, be accountable, and act as owners.

Information is what you give people to help them do their job. Communication is how you energize people to move the ball down the court. People need two things from you: clear, specific, and unequivocal direction and positive inspiration. You must deliver both. Providing one without the other does not work.

How can you inspire positive action with every message? Aren't some messages simply straightforward information? The answer is "no," not if you are a leader who communicates accountably. Remember, there are two parts to every message: what you intend to say and what listeners hear. Just by adding a simple phrase, an information-only message can change into an inspirational one.

Short Statements That Inspire Positive Action

Speaking Accountably

- "That's the problem in a nutshell."
  Add: *"Now it's **up to us** to turn this around."*

- "This is an issue we must address quickly."
  Add: *"I'm **confident we can** do this."*

- "We will meet on Friday at 8 a.m. in the conference room."
  Add: *"Let's use this time to generate **new ideas together**."*

- "I haven't had a chance to read your report."
  Add: *"I always **appreciate** how you look at things."*

- "We are facing a number of challenges this next year."
  Add: *"I'm happy to be on a great team. We'll need everyone's thinking and energy."*

- "Good morning."
  Add: *"It's always good to see you."*

- "Here's the document. Read it and let's talk."
  Add: *"I'm interested in hearing your thoughts."*

Why it works: It doesn't take much. It may be just a brief statement that allows you to connect with the person or provide positive direction for an upcoming meeting. The point is to focus on inspiring positive action rather than on providing information. When you do this, small changes in how you communicate will make a big difference.

To inspire positive action you must ask first, What message do I want to send and second, How do I want people to feel? When you inspire others, they experience new ways of thinking, feeling, and acting. With your words alone you can help people feel connected to a larger group and mission. You will also help people develop a personal connection with you as their leader. This is a value that leaders often underestimate.

> Answer these two questions *before* you speak:
> *What message do I want to send?*
> *How do I want people to feel?*

People move forward and results are produced when you inspire action in others. The direction is backward when you treat communication as a task or simple information transfer. What you say and how you say it are your primary vehicles for making things happen.

The Reason Managers and Leaders Exist

Why are managers and leaders necessary? Your obvious role is to produce business results, but how is that done? The simple answer is *through people.* Your responsibility is to bring new realities into existence—to make something happen that would not happen otherwise. Leaders are not hired to manage the status quo. Your role is to move people and the organization forward toward specific outcomes. People are a major factor in the equation of success for a leader. When it comes right down to it, managers and leaders exist to create an environment in which people excel.

Leaders and organizations committed to 100% accountability need to look carefully at the message that is sent by words and behavior. Ask yourself:

- What message is sent when organizations retain and promote leaders who produce strong bottom-line results but alienate and damage people?

- What results could organizations produce with leaders who inspire people *and* produce strong bottom-line results?

How can leaders keep people moving forward in a world of constant change? They must provide what is missing and needed. People want and need a sense of belonging, a feeling of connection to a larger group, a greater purpose. If they did not have this need, they would be working on their own. But because working with other people fuels the soul and reinvents the feeling of family, people often choose organizations over individual work. Some have tried going it alone, only to discover that being a lone ranger is lonely and uninspiring.

> *Leaders are accountable for creating an environment in which people can excel.*

It is the responsibility of leaders to create an environment in which people can excel. But there is something more at stake for you and your organization: sustainable competitive advantage. Competitive advantage used to revolve around market dominance, size, and a respected name. Today flexibility and swift response are vital to success. This is where people come into the equation. People who are flexible, adjust to change quickly, and take ownership and accountability provide companies with a sustainable, strategic, competitive advantage. People make the difference. Your competitors cannot copy the esprit de corps you create in your group or organization. They cannot duplicate your culture or environment. This is what will set you and your company apart—the fire in your people.

Bring out the best in your people by creating an environment that

- Is safe and open, where people feel free to speak up without fear of repercussions

- Produces extraordinary business results through the inspiration of its people

- Is fun, high-energy, and collaborative where people enjoy working together

- Is the envy of others and gives you a sustainable competitive advantage

People want to make a difference. With inspired leadership, people will give tremendous effort. Your job as a leader is to communicate in a way that inspires positive action in others—not occasionally, but all the time. Communicating accountably increases trust and credibility and dramatically reduces communication breakdowns, costly mistakes, and disappointment in people. Most importantly, you will increase morale and performance. But in order to do this, you must be willing to focus on how others respond to what you say, not on what you intended to say. Strong leaders are willing to measure their effectiveness by the impact they have on others. Accountable communication allows you to engage the boundless energy of people.

The Changing Language of Twenty-First-Century Leaders

About every decade or so, words change in the business world. One decade the focus is on quality, the next on reengineering and empowerment. Words come and go. But when they are introduced, they have specific meaning and provide important distinctions. Language defines reality, and it is important for leaders to stay ahead of the curve and use language that motivates people to think in different ways. The changing language of the twenty-first century is reflected in how a new language has replaced old and quaint words. See the box 'The Changing Language of Twenty-First-Century Leaders.' It is clear that this century has begun with a major emphasis on accountability and integrity. But words have no meaning until people create it. The first step is to replace old words with the new language of the twenty-first century. The next step is to bring these words to life and provide meaning and application for your day-to-day workplace. As you read each chapter, you will find numerous ways to apply and integrate the communication skills so that 100% accountability becomes a way of life.

The Changing Language of Twenty-First-Century Leaders

Quaint Relics	**New Language**
• Entitlement	• Accountability
• Loyalty	• Portable career assets
• Training and retraining	• Lifelong learning and personal growth
• Follow the rules; comply and obey	• Make the rules; be an owner
• Protection and financial security	• Marketability

- Status and command rights
- Relationship and partnership privileges

- Commitment to the company
- Commitment to high standards

- Continuity and consistency
- Constant change as a way of life

- Improving and getting better
- Making quantum leaps and changes

- Customer satisfaction
- Customer accountability

The new language of this century will lead you in the right direction—creating an environment of accountability where people can succeed. To create a climate where people feel safe to speak up and produce results leaders must manage the impact of their communication. Words are extremely powerful, but unharnessed they can be deadly. Undirected words run amuck and wreak havoc everywhere. They have either no target or the wrong target. You never know how or where these deadly words are going to land and how they are going to impact people. The price you pay for their unpredictability and inconsistent results is rework, rework, and more rework.

Unharnessed words have the power to wipe out months and years of work in a single moment. They are so powerful that they can damage relationships and build permanent walls between people. They have the power to derail an entire organization and send morale in a downward spiral. They can eliminate goodwill and any extra effort that individuals choose to give. Unharnessed words can freeze the action and paralyze people. Enormous amounts of time and energy will have to be used by leaders to recover the spirit of people, if recovery is even possible.

Are You Accountable for the Impact of Your Words?

- **Avoid:** *"You're acting ridiculous. How can you expect me to respond to a question that has absolutely no logic to it and doesn't relate to anything we're talking about?"*

Why it doesn't work: When you are disappointed, unhappy, or dissatisfied with the behavior of an individual, it is best not to use the word *you* as the first word in the sentence. It acts as a wagging finger, pointing and attacking the person. Using the word *ridiculous* coupled with the phrase *absolutely no logic* will evoke defensiveness in most people. The result? The individual will either fight back or retreat—neither of which is productive for resolving issues.

- **Replace with:** *"I'm having difficulty understanding how what you're saying connects to the issue we're discussing. Would you please explain . . . ?"*

Why it works: The leader starts with his or her experience by saying, "I'm having difficulty understanding." Listen to the difference between saying, "I'm having difficulty understanding" and "You're being ridiculous." When you accept accountability for how something is impacting you rather than attacking the other person, you get a better response and higher-quality information. Additionally, the request to connect the topics is direct and puts the focus on clarifying rather than on defending.

In contrast, harnessed words are accountable. They are directed energy that is focused on a specific target with great clarity and determination. These words inspire positive action in people, moving them forward to accomplish specific goals. Harnessed words are workhorses—strong, reliable, and predictable in the results they produce. Harnessing the power of words replaces quantity with quality. Messages are precise, clear, and straightforward, eliminating many unnecessary words that get in the way.

Do You Trigger Action or Reaction?

- **Avoid:** *"Everyone needs to get on board fast to handle this mess."*

Why it doesn't work: The finger is pointed at others with the word everyone. This noninclusive language has conveniently eliminated the leader from being part of the solution. Additionally, the word mess is a judgment that can trigger a negative reaction.

- **Replace with:** *"I need everyone on board fast. I can't do this alone. Together we can turn this situation around."*

Why it works: With subtle changes alone, the meaning and impact of the message are changed. The use of the word *we* includes the leader and others who can face the problem together. Self-disclosure statements such as, "I can't do this alone" make the leader human and someone people can relate to and understand. Finally, the words used are neutral and focus on the facts thereby needing no interpretation.

When a message is direct and on point, people respond with energy, enthusiasm, and commitment. Accountable words maximize understanding and reduce confusion; this is something leaders constantly strive to do. The unwavering commitment and strength of your message now replace the struggle for clarity and focus. When people can count on consistent, reliable direction from you and know exactly what you expect, they will climb mountains. Your clarity of purpose, the reliability of your message, and your ability to inspire people daily, rather than as a random event, make morale soar and performance skyrocket.

People are your most important asset, and words are your most powerful vehicle for unleashing the best in them. What you say and how you say it determines not only the results produced by people but also directly impacts your career. Harness the power of words rather than allowing automatic and habitual patterns to get you in trouble. The most important goal for a leader is to deliver messages that inspire positive action in others—every time. Your goal is to learn how to replace ineffective and damaging words with accountable communication. Leaders who make things happen through the power of their words are leaders who rise to the top.

The power of random words is not only diffused but also often damaging. Let's say you've just listened to a meeting presentation by a peer. Not only do you disagree with what she just said but you're also quick to speak up with the first thing that pops into your head:

"*I completely disagree.*" Your communication may be an accurate reflection of what you are feeling, but let's match it against our criteria for accountable communication: Will this message move people forward or backward? You already know the answer to this question. The statement "I completely disagree" is emotionally charged, and people typically react to it as an attack. The situation could easily escalate to a level where no resolution is possible.

Engaging people at both the intellectual and emotional levels inspires action. Remember that there are only two directions your speaking takes people—forward or backward. This simple concept is one that makes all the difference when it comes to inspiring people.

Do You Inspire or Derail People?

- **Avoid:** *"I've made a decision to move ahead with a program that will help us achieve better performance."*

Why it doesn't work: "I've made a decision" sounds pretty much like lone-ranger language. People will typically sit on the sidelines and "wait and see" if the leader's idea is more than a flash in the pan. The word *program* is used to present the idea. It sounds limiting and temporary. A program is an event or a destination. If the leader is attempting to enroll people in a major change effort, this language is not going to do it. Besides, the people have nothing to do with the decision and so what if they achieve better performance? That doesn't sound too exciting.

- **Replace with:** *"I see a possibility for us to be the first group to lead the way in building a high-performance organization. I know we can accomplish this together."*

Why it works: The leader starts by sharing a vision statement: "I see a possibility for . . . ," followed by a statement about being number one. Whether it is being number one or being the best, everyone wants to have a purpose that gets them excited each morning. Being on a winning team is compelling. The leader also expresses his or her belief in the group and underscores how they will accomplish this together.

When you communicate in a meaningful way, you also benefit your own career. Leaders who know how to mobilize a group, team, or organization are rare and in high demand. Every company seeks leaders who have strong people skills and who can inspire others. Your expertise, whether it is in the fields of finance, law, technology, or engineering, got you where you are today. Learn to inspire action in others and you will continue to move forward. Saying it right the first time is the key.

Key Communication Principles

Principle 1: Accountable communication inspires positive action in others.

Think Twice. Communication is not the transfer of information. People want to be inspired, and meaningful dialogue is what engages and energizes people.

Action. Keep a close watch on how you speak both at work and at home. Do you inspire positive action when you speak? If not, you may be focusing on your agenda rather than on the individual.

Principle 2: The most powerful person is the most flexible one.

Think Twice. Flexibility provides you with options. The greater your flexibility in thinking and learning, the stronger your leadership. Demonstrating flexibility and giving up an "I know" attitude tells others you are human and let's them connect with you on a personal level.

Action. Examine your life to discover where you are inflexible. Where have you established rigid patterns of thinking, speaking, and behaving? Then choose a pattern you want to break and see what new possibilities are created.

Principle 3: Speaking is an action that moves the conversation forward or backward.

Think Twice. What you say has the power to move people forward or derail them. There is no such thing as standing still. When you communicate, your words are either accountable or off-track.

Action. Pay close attention to your words. Watch the reaction of others and the consequences. Often, these reactions may be hard to gauge at first. If you spend time repairing damage or repeating the same message, consider the reason. If action is not moving forward, what needs to be altered in your message?

Principle 4: The reason managers and leaders exist is to create an environment in which people can excel.

Think Twice. You are not hired to manage the status quo. You are there to move the action forward and make things happen. You are there to make a difference.

Action. Create an environment to bring out the best in people by inspiring positive action on a daily basis. Look for ways to add a short inspirational statement, such as "It's always great to get your input." Add this to the end of a conversation or memo; it will leave the person feeling energized and connected.

2

The Key to
the Kingdom

How to Capture Discretionary Effort and Build Accountability

Your Purpose

To unleash the extra effort of people by dealing with **resignation** and building **accountability**.

Resignation is the single biggest problem in our workforce today. And resignation looks like apathy! It's an obvious mistake. They (people) look apathetic, but they're really resigned. Apathetic is when *they* don't care. Resignation is when they think *you* don't care. Big difference!

Mike Beason
"You're an Inspiration—NOT,"
California@Work Newsjournal

In a perfect world, employees work at their maximum capacity. Pep talks and morale boosters are unnecessary since everyone is giving 110 percent. In this world, worrying about how you say something is pointless since nothing is misunderstood. Unfortunately, we don't live in a perfect world and what we say is critical. We need to be accountable at all times. When a leader's words and actions continually evoke negative reactions from people, the results are resignation, hopelessness, and despair.

This is the story of Brian—a glimpse into the life of an employee who once was highly accountable and now is disillusioned and resigned.

Brian is a hard worker who produces great results. He is the last of a dying breed—an employee who has been with the company for more than 20 years. Everyone likes him; he is positive, upbeat, and bright. But over the years things have changed. Before, he felt he was part of a winning team, but no more. Now when he listens to his boss and senior management speak, he feels they only care about results, not the people who produce them.

Brian's feeling of resignation caused him to shrink. It started with his thoughts and then moved into his behaviors. Rather than think about what was possible, he thought only of what was not possible. Instead of acting as an owner, he behaved as a victim. He stopped listening to the empty promises of management. He stopped trusting the words managers used to pump up the troops. Finally, he narrowed his focus to only his areas of responsibility.

Brian's disappointments grew over time until he found himself in a deep state of resignation. Today, he feels hopeless and believes management will never change. He talks to fewer people, avoids team projects, and works alone. His natural energy and enthusiasm have been replaced with caution and skepticism. Brian no longer gives any extra effort to get the job done. He used to have a purpose: Now he only has a job.

When you ignore resignation or deny that it exists, three things happen: (1) Morale goes down, (2) accountability diminishes, and (3) discretionary effort disappears altogether. When people are resigned, they give only what they have to give in order to avoid unpleasant consequences.

> When **resignation** is high, **morale** is low.
> Count on it.

Discretionary Effort:
What People Are Willing to Give

There are a lot of resigned employees in the workforce today just like Brian: people with tremendous ability, a sense of loyalty, and a strong work ethic. However, they expend only the necessary effort to get the job done. Their discretionary effort, the effort above and beyond what their job requires, is withheld.

> ### Discretionary Effort
> *The extra effort people* **choose** *to give that cannot be mandated by a leader or organization.*

When economists use the term *discretionary income*, they are referring to income that is left over after people pay their fixed and neces-

sary expenses. Discretionary income is what the individual can control. A parallel concept exists in the business world, and it is called *discretionary effort*. This is the portion of effort that is controlled by the
individual and cannot be mandated by a leader or an organization.

The results of a survey of the U.S. workforce on discretionary
effort are staggering. Most people invest about 60 percent of what
they are capable of in order to receive a good performance review. The
remaining 40 percent is discretionary: It is that extra effort that people choose to give when they feel inspired. When people are unenthused, they give the minimum amount of effort to their job to avoid
being penalized or fired.

This is in direct conflict with what people really want and need.
People want a purpose of sufficient magnitude to feel energized and
inspired. They have an inner need to give their best. The amount of
discretionary effort released is directly tied to the ability of leaders to
engage people in meaningful dialogue.

How to Spot Resignation

What exactly is resignation? It is the belief that people and circumstances are hopelessly fixed and unchangeable. The most common
remark from people who are resigned is "Things will never change
here." To them, everything and everyone appear to be unalterable.
Unmet expectations and cumulative disappointments sow the seeds
of resignation. When people no longer find their job or leaders compelling, purpose is lost and resignation takes over.

When people are resigned, they continue to be responsible for
their job, but the feeling of personal accountability for overall business results vanishes. Signs of resignation are avoidance, lack of

involvement, unenthusiastic compliance, a wait-and-see attitude, and the absence of urgency.

The most insidious aspect of resignation is its ability to spread and contaminate others. Resignation is like a virus. A handful of resigned individuals can easily grow into a resigned group or organization. Skeptical and disappointed people seek out sympathetic others. They also plant seeds of discontent and negative thinking in people who are otherwise satisfied with their jobs and company.

What Resigned Employees Say

- "Nothing is ever going to change here, especially management!"

- "This is just another program-of-the-month."

- "Senior management never listens."

- "Wait and see. This will pass."

- "It won't make any difference."

- "I'll just do my job."

- "Ignore them and they'll go away."

- "Another 'go get 'em' speech from the CEO. Does she really think we care?"

- "I've done my part. Let them do the rest."

- "Just pretend you agree. Then we'll do what we want."

Why it doesn't work: This language reflects the following attitudes of resigned employees: (1) wait and see, (2) comply, (3) avoid, (4) resist, or (5) tolerate.

Hallway conversations are underground conversations that employees have with everyone but you. You are the last to hear what is really going on. The only effective method for spotting resignation is to notice what people are *not* saying. Pay attention to what is missing and *not* being said or expressed. Here are some clues: When people are resigned they do not talk about their (1) commitment to goals, targets, or initiatives; (2) accountability for their impact on people and results; or (3) partnering and collaborating with others, especially with you and other leaders.

The obvious absence of the "language of accountability" tells the story. What people do *not* say is as important as what they say. When it comes to accountability, you want people to speak in a positive manner that moves the action forward. The notable lack of accountability language is a sure sign that inspiration is missing and resignation is present.

What Inspired Employees Say

- "I will, I promise, I commit, I agree to deliver, you can count on . . ."

- "I'm accountable, I'm responsible, I accept personal accountability, I'm up for taking charge of . . ."

- "We can, we will, my partners, my team, our group, together . . ."

Why it works: People verbally articulate the future they want by speaking in a positive, assertive, and compelling manner. To spot resignation, notice what people do *not* say. When you do not hear people speaking about their commitment, accountability, and partnership, consider this a strong signal that resignation is alive and well.

Shrinking the Game—What People Do When They Are Resigned

Business has all the elements of a game: rules, scoreboard, players, coaches, and owners. People are either "in the game" or "on the sideline." Shrinking the game is a natural, protective response from people who are resigned. When people believe they are limited, not valued, or not heard, they guard their investment of energy in the organization. This happens every day in the business world and applies to highly successful, hard-working, and talented people. They continue to produce outstanding results, but only in their defined areas of responsibility. Ownership, accountability, and a big-picture perspective are missing. When resigned, people move off the field and onto the sidelines.

What causes a person to shrink? It is triggered by something that happens, comments by an individual with power, or a series of events that happen over time and result in disillusionment and disappointment. The feelings of dissatisfaction accumulate and build. People file them away only to show their resentment of leadership in their behaviors.

How People Feel When They Are Resigned

- Small
- Unvalued
- Insignificant

- Unappreciated
- Unimportant
- Unneeded

The shrinking process is complete when a person believes "This is just the way things are. Nothing is ever going to change here." People work hard and produce results but fall far short of what is possible. But when discretionary effort is put forth: watch out. People go far beyond what is necessary or required and produce unpredictable results.

The lack of inspiration and accountability directly impacts business results including productivity, innovation, and efficiency. How people feel has a direct impact on how they execute. Human capital is one of your primary concerns as a leader. To produce consistent outstanding results, you must consistently inspire positive action in others.

Your goal is to get people off the sidelines and back into the game. Use words that create possibility, expand thinking, and tear down limiting beliefs about what is not possible. You are their coach. You are the person who focuses their efforts and raises their spirits. You are the one who holds the key to making the impossible happen through people working together.

Getting Others Back in the Game
Speaking Accountably

- "Times are tough. So what? We can turn this around."
- "We've faced challenges before. We can do it again."
- "We're accountable for the future and we will deliver."
- "Just because it hasn't been done doesn't mean we can't do it."
- "We need new thinking."
- "Generate new possibilities."
- "Take it apart and find a better way."
- "Focus on what we want, not what we don't want."
- "Create the future you want; don't get stuck in the past."
- "Think outside the box."
- "Do something different."
- "Think in different categories."
- "Anything can be changed."
- "Just do it."
- "Change it."

- "Reinvent it."

- "Make it happen."

Why it works: These phrases challenge people to make things happen in spite of constant change or tough circumstances. By demanding positive action, these words place accountability on the individual or group to deliver results.

People want to believe that they make a difference, that there is possibility. They want hope, a compelling future, and a purpose that demands their greatest efforts. And just as important, they want to know that problems and circumstances are not insurmountable. These assurances need to come from you—that everything is going to be okay. And you need to say it with conviction not once, but over and over again.

When *You* Shrink the Game

It is not uncommon for leaders and managers to be resigned. In fact, successful people are frequently resigned. It's just harder to spot because it is well camouflaged. Before you deny that you are resigned, think about this: Are you giving and doing your best? Are you at the top of your game? Are you inspired every day when you come to work? Wouldn't you want your people to answer these questions with a resounding "yes"? Can *you*?

What complicates the answer to this question is the fact that you work hard and produce superior results. Your performance reviews are consistently strong. But is there something missing for you? Only you know the answer to this question. You know what it feels like to be in the "zone," to be turned on and enthused by endless ideas, thoughts, and inventions of your mind. You know what it is to give 100 percent effort. Others will not be able to tell if you are operating at 80 percent or 100 percent. But you will know the difference.

Take a moment and answer the following questions. They focus on the behaviors of accountability and what you model for others. These questions are thought-provoking and are intended to cause you to reflect on two issues: Where are you shrinking the game? and Do you model accountability in both your speaking and actions? Answer the questions with a "yes" or "no." If you are not sure, the response is "no."

1. **Are you inspired?** Are you inspired about your job, what you are doing, the company, the overall mission, purpose, and the people (including people senior to you)?

2. **Are you disappointed?** Do you feel let down? Are you skeptical and untrusting of peers and/or people senior to you?

3. **When you are disappointed or resigned, do you take immediate action to deal with the situation?** Do you recognize when you are resigned? Do you deny or attempt to suppress your feelings? Where are you shrinking the game?

4. **Do you accept 100% accountability for your impact on business results and others?** Do you accept accountability rather than blaming others?

5. **Do you hold yourself accountable for the "best in performance"?** Do you deliver the best in performance even in the face of challenging circumstances? When you are not at your best, do you take immediate, corrective action?

6. **Do you hold others accountable for their "best in performance"?** Do you hold coworkers, subordinates, superiors, and peers accountable for consistent, outstanding performance?

7. **Do others consider you to be a collaborative team player?** Do people enjoy working with you? Do people want you on their team? Would you want to be on your team?

What did you learn? Did you discover areas in which you are disappointed or resigned? Your speaking and actions reflect how you feel and think. What you say offers clues about whether you are resigned. More to the point, how you talk causes others to shrink the game. People listen carefully to what you say and what you do not say. Your silence speaks as loudly as your words. If senior management announces a major initiative and you avoid talking about it with employees, you send a strong message. Accurate or not, what they hear by your silence is your lack of support for senior management's initiative.

When *You* Shrink the Game
Speaking That Derails

- "They told me and now I'm telling you."

- "That's the way they want it."

- "That's the way it is."

- "What initiative? Oh yeah, that one."

- "You can't change it and neither can I."

- "Don't rock the boat."

- "Just do your job. That's what I'm doing."

- "Don't get carried away with that 'change' stuff. Focus on your job."

- "Forget about it; there's nothing that can be done."

- "Nothing's going to change. Stick with what you know."

- "There's no point in questioning this; it is what it is."

- "Let's just get to work and do the best we can in spite of . . ."

- "I'm not excited about this either, but it's what they want."

Why it doesn't work: When leaders are resigned it shows up in several ways: (1) we/they speaking—dividing into camps, (2) dismissing initiatives and changing efforts, (3) begrudgingly maintaining the status quo, and (4) reducing focus to smaller areas of concern. These words shrink the game for everyone on the playing field, including you. Ultimately they kill possibility, hope, and the future.

People only do what their leaders are willing to do. Your level of accountability determines the actions of others. Leadership means leading the way. Your behavior and communication tell others what you expect from them. It is no different than being a parent. If you want your children to become responsible adults, you must demonstrate and model responsibility in your actions. If you want your employees to raise the bar on accountability and performance, you must lead the way. If you want your workplace free of resignation, start by discovering where *you* are resigned.

When a leader is resigned, it has a domino effect that kills the spirit of a lot of other people. When leaders and managers are resigned, this is the death knell of an organization.

Talking to Your Boss When You Are Resigned
Speaking Accountably

- YOU: "I'm struggling with something that's bothering me about how we work together. Are you open to talking about this?"

Why it works: Your first statement tells your boss you are struggling (not closed or decided) and states the topic—how the two of you work together. Next, you ask if he or she is willing to talk. The question gives your listener time to process what you said and shift gears. In this regard the question "Are you open to talking about this?" is rhetorical, since few people would respond with a "no."

- YOU: "Last week when we reviewed my performance, I walked away feeling disappointed. I'm disappointed in myself for not delivering what you want and not providing the input and information you need to review my work."

Why it works: This is a place where "I" language is appropriate and necessary. By using the word *I*, you take personal accountability. Rather than pointing the finger and blaming your boss for your disappointment, you accept accountability for how you feel. In the above statement you acknowledge your boss's concern (i.e., unacceptable performance) and open the door for correcting the situation by providing additional information.

- You: "I failed to give you critical information about what I've been working on with 'X.' I'd like to correct this now. Would you be willing to listen?"

Why it works: You take accountability (not blame) for the situation. You also provide a solution and ask for a commitment to listen. Asking people if they are willing to listen is an acceptable request to most people. It frees their mind to hear what you are saying rather than sort what you say into "agree" or "disagree" categories.

Talking to People Who Are Resigned and Skeptical

Resigned people search for evidence to validate and support their beliefs. Unknowingly, you provide them with what they want. For example, you announce a new program that provides employees with flex time to accommodate family and personal needs. It sounds like a benefit. But those who are resigned see it as a form of manipulation by you and other members of management. Instead of seeing the positive aspects, they may view flex time as a way to keep them quiet about bigger issues such as competitive salaries.

This underscores a fundamental element in resignation—people interpret everything you say to support their viewpoint. If they don't trust management, what you say will be heard and interpreted as evidence that you are untrustworthy. Every time you open your mouth, you provide "proof" that you don't really care about people.

When you avoid dealing with resignation, it takes much longer to uncover the real issues. Trying to gloss over resignation with incentives and rewards often results in talented people leaving the organization or, worse, they stay and infect others. In the meantime it doesn't matter what you say because you can't say it right. The only way to win is to deal with resignation directly. Talking to people about how they feel and encouraging them to express their concerns bring issues to the surface where they can effectively be resolved. A straightforward approach is the only approach that will turn people around. The words and phrases you use have the ability to get people off the sidelines and back into the game.

Start by dealing with the real problem—how people feel—and ignore the symptoms. When the actual problem is resolved, symptoms disappear on their own. Read on to learn a simple three-step process to take the emotional charge out of a conversation.

Dealing with Emotionally Charged People

Step 1: Stop discussing the content and switch to the process.

Step 2: Separate the symptoms from the problem.

Step 3: Validate all feelings.

Step 1: Stop Discussing the Content and Switch to the Process

When a person is emotionally charged, immediately stop discussing the content. Let's say you sit down to discuss an upcoming reorganization with a direct report. He is not thinking about reorganization; he is thinking about a disturbing memo that you sent a few days ago. You forgot all about the memo; he has not. He seems uptight, a little clipped and abrupt. You chalk it up to stress and ignore it. You begin the discussion and suddenly—Wham! Out of the blue, he charges and attacks your plan for reorganization.

Your first reaction may be to strike back, but wait. You missed the first set of cues: Do not miss this one. All you know at this point is that he is reacting. You do not know what is causing the reaction. You think he is reacting to your reorganization plan because that's what he is attacking. You are at a critical juncture. Do not take communication literally. When people are emotionally charged, they react to the first thing that comes into their line of sight. It is frequently not the real issue.

What should you do? Stop discussing the content (the reorganization) and talk about the process (how you are communicating with one another). A process discussion includes talking about your relationship and any unexpressed thoughts, concerns, and feelings.

> Do not take communication literally.
> When people are **emotionally charged**, they react to the first thing that comes into their line of sight.
> It is seldom the REAL issue.

Having a conversation about content on top of an emotional charge does not work. It taints the discussion, interferes with problem resolution, produces bad solutions, and, most predictably, results in arguing about the wrong issues. Let's look at a better way to handle this:

Uncover the "Real" Problem

Speaking Accountably

YOUR DIRECT REPORT: "There's no way this plan is going to fly! I won't ask my people to do this."

YOU: "Something's really bothering you. Let's set the discussion on reorganization aside and talk about what's going on with you. Is it something I have said or done?"

Why it works: You stop the discussion on reorganization. This is a good idea since you notice the reaction of your direct report is out of proportion for the topic. By switching the conversation to the process of communication—how you are talking to one another—you can uncover the real issue. You take accountability (not blame) by asking, "Is it something I have said or done?" This makes it safe for the individual to respond in a straightforward manner.

Step 2: Separate the Symptoms from the Problem

Pep talks, perks, incentives, or new opportunities are a manager's arsenal for solving problems. They seldom work. This approach treats the symptoms, not the problems. People comply with what you want, but continue to harbor resentment. Compliance is not the same as alignment. People who comply—instead of committing and aligning with you—unconsciously erode your efforts at every opportunity.

Remember the story of Brian at the beginning of this chapter? Let's see what happens when his boss comes into the picture.

> Brian's boss notices his performance is slipping. She calls him into her office and delivers a lengthy pep talk on how to improve his work. Brian does not bother to respond; there's no need since she's doing all the talking. Instead of feeling inspired, he feels even more misunderstood.

Now read the two approaches below where Brian's boss opens the conversation. Which approach targets the symptoms and which focuses on the real issue?

- **Approach 1:** "Your last project was two days late and, frankly, it was very disappointing. What's going on?"

- **Approach 2:** "You're always focused and on task, but lately you seem preoccupied. What's on your mind? Maybe I can help."

The first approach focuses on the symptom: poor performance. Attempting to solve symptoms only compounds the situation. People are frustrated because the problem is unresolved. Brian needs his boss to listen to how he feels. What he receives instead is communication that is off-track. His boss ignores his resignation and focuses solely on performance.

In the second approach, his boss focuses on a behavioral change she has noticed. Brian is normally focused and on time. Lately he has been preoccupied and is missing his deadlines. By talking about these changes, the manager begins to search for the real problem. The second approach hits the target: The *problem* is resignation; the *symptom* is performance.

Step 3: Validate All Feelings

When people believe they are unfairly criticized or judged, they suppress their resentment and route it in unproductive directions such as talking to others. A caveat: Just because you do not hear about issues, concerns, or disappointments does not mean they do not exist. Since you are the last person to hear anything, never trust the obvious.

Validating Feelings

Avoid:	**Replace with:**
• How can you feel this way?	• I didn't realize you were feeling this way.
• I can't believe you're saying this.	• I'm glad you're telling me your concerns.
• That's not true. You know better than this.	• You have a valid and different experience than mine. I want to understand what's going on for you. Please tell me more.
• You shouldn't feel like this.	• It's all right. Whatever you're feeling is okay. I just want to understand.

- You're overreacting.

- This is really bothering you. I've obviously missed something that is very important to you. Talk to me.

It is important to validate how people feel without necessarily agreeing with their solutions. Feelings are not right or wrong, good or bad. They are internal sensations. The best thing to do when dealing with an emotionally charged individual is to encourage the person to fully express. Then listen and validate. Do not judge and criticize. Your focus is to understand what the individual is feeling and not assess whether or not he or she *should* have these feelings.

What can you do when you don't have time to walk through the three-step process? You can address the resignation by letting the individual know you recognize something is bothering him or her and you want to talk about it as soon as possible. Do not ignore resignation or attempt to move past it by trying to cheer someone up. This results in the person not feeling heard or understood. Now you have two problems—resistance *and* resignation.

Dealing with Resignation
When You Are Short on Time
Speaking Accountably

- "I can tell something is bothering you. I don't have time now but can we talk later today? I want to understand."

- "We need to deal with this business issue now, but I notice you seem preoccupied; something is on your mind. Let's meet for lunch tomorrow so we can really talk. How you are doing is important to me."

- "We only have 20 minutes to put the finishing touches on this report. I want you to know I care about how you're doing with this merger. Let's set up a time to meet this week."

Why it works: Three elements make each of the above statements work.

1. Make an observation about the person's behavior such as "I can tell something is bothering you." The observations are purposely broad and general rather than labeling (e.g., "you look angry"). Labels, accurate or not, tend to provoke reactions.

2. Let the person know you do not have time to talk now, but you will make time. Recognize that how far out in time you schedule the meeting will tell the person how important the conversation is to you.

3. Make a relationship statement such as "You are important to me."

The secret to getting people to fully express is to ask a final question when they least expect it. After they have said everything they have to say, pause and ask: "Is there anything else you would like to tell me?" Both your pause and question allow the mind to search one final time for what has not been said. Often it's the most important thing.

> ## Ask One Final Question after Everything Has Been Said:
> *"Is there anything else you would like to tell me?"*

Since a handful of resigned individuals can easily grow into a resigned group or organization, it is imperative that you stop the growth in its early stages. You need to get people off the sidelines and back into the game. And the way to do this is by using words that create possibility and expand thinking. You are the coach, the person who focuses efforts and raises spirits. Resignation and skepticism are a normal part of business life. People move out of the game and onto the sidelines, taking their enthusiasm with them. Resignation is not something that disappears forever.

It takes a dedicated coach who is willing to deal with the human side in order to engage people at top levels of performance. The spirit of an organization is contained in how much discretionary effort people are willing to give. Your willingness and skill in dealing with the real problem and not the symptoms allow you to get people back in the game, which will generate rewarding results. You hold the key to making the impossible happen by inspiring positive action in others.

Key Communication Principles

Principle 1: Turn hallway conversations into public dialogues.

Think Twice. You are the last person to hear about what is going on. Remember this, and you will not be surprised or blindsided. Private conversations, often referred to as underground or hallway discussions, occur all the time. They are dialogues where selected others are excluded, usually management. People engage in these discussions with everyone except the person who can resolve the issue or concern. These exchanges can fester and grow into resignation.

Action. Be on the hunt for underground conversations. When you discover an underground conversation, talk about it in a constructive, open manner. Make these "undiscussable" topics a priority for both individual and group meetings.

Principle 2: Do not take communication literally when talking with an emotionally charged person.

Think Twice. When people are emotionally charged, they react to the first thing that comes into their line of sight; it is seldom the real problem. Don't react to the first issue presented and steer clear of trying to provide solutions. Your job is to listen and understand until the emotional charge has dissipated. Then you can problem solve, not before.

Action. Observe your reaction to a person who is emotionally charged. Do you have an overwhelming urge to solve the problem? If you do, work on listening to understand. Avoid providing any solutions until the individual asks for your thoughts.

Principle 3: Treat the problem and ignore the symptoms.

Think Twice. Symptoms frequently camouflage the real problem. When you treat a symptom, the problem occurs over and over again.

A tip-off that you are dealing with symptoms and not the real issue is when numerous concerns are presented. A typical response would be to say, "Let's take these one at a time." Don't! This will lead you into a maze. Even if you solve every complaint on the list, the person will still be unhappy and dissatisfied because the real issue has not been addressed.

Action

1. When you hear multiple concerns, ask yourself, "What larger problem do these symptoms suggest or indicate?" This is called "chunking up" and moves the discussion from specifics to the larger concern.

2. In responding to numerous concerns ask, "What's really bothering you? It must be something very important to you." Express authentic concern, for example, "This must be difficult for you."

Principle 4: Validate feelings—if you argue with them, you'll lose.

Think Twice. Feelings are valid and need to be respected. You cannot talk someone out of how he or she feels nor can you use logic to convince him or her to feel otherwise. The only solution is to validate feelings by listening and understanding. Feelings are real for the person who has them. Serious relationship problems occur when people believe their feelings are minimized, judged, or invalidated. The key is to support an individual without agreeing with them.

Action

1. When someone tells you how he or she feels, immediately validate the feelings. Say, "You're really concerned," or, "This is really bothering you."

2. Prompt the individual to express. Say, "I want to understand everything. Please go on."

Principle 5: Fix the problem, not the blame.

Think Twice. Focus on the problem, not who caused it. People will help you solve a problem even when they are the problem as long as they are not the targets of blame. Finger-pointing or implying blame produces embarrassment, shame, and regret—emotions that are difficult from which to recover. People do not want to let you down.

Action

1. The next time you encounter a problem or breakdown, ask, "What do we need to do to correct this situation?" instead of "Who dropped the ball on this one?"

2. Focus on prevention by asking, "How can we stop this from happening again?" instead of "What are you going to do to make sure this never happens again?"

3

Your Power, Your Position, and Its Impact

How to Gain Trust and Create Alignment

Your Purpose

To transform symbolic power into real power by gaining trust and creating alignment.

———————

Power must be the servant, not the master.

Michael Korda
Power: How to Get It, How to Use It

One night a ship's captain out at sea observed what seemed to be the lights of another ship. He had his first mate signal the other ship. "Change your course 10 degrees south," the captain demanded. The reply came back, "Change your course 10 degrees north." The ship's captain, annoyed with having his order disregarded, answered, "I am a captain. Change *your* course 10 degrees south." To which he received the reply, "I am a seaman first class and I say change your course 10 degrees north." Infuriated by the obvious lack of respect and deference to his position and power, the captain signaled back, "Darn it, man, I say change *your* course 10 degrees south. I'm on a battleship." The reply came back without delay, "I say change *your* course 10 degrees north. I'm in a lighthouse."

In the story, the captain assumes two things—his power is supreme and others must comply with his requests beyond question. The seaman quietly notes the arrogance of the captain and continues the conversation until the real situation is revealed. Ultimately the captain looks foolish. He has been ordering a lighthouse to move— a visual image that is both ludicrous and comical. Of course, you could argue that the captain did not know it was a lighthouse, but this is precisely the point. Leaders are accountable for dealing with accurate information. Poor decisions are often the result of low-quality information and false assumptions.

The captain's need to be right and all-powerful results in three things: (1) He makes false assumptions, (2) he is positional and intractable when he does not receive the proper respect and deference, and (3) he repeats the same order over and over again, using declarative statements. Did you notice the captain never asked a question? By using declarative statements to the exclusion of questions, it sends a message that the need to be right is stronger than the need to understand.

Power blinds people to the obvious. It is like an intoxicating drink, stimulating the senses while destroying the ability to think. Those with power do not usually understand what is happening to them. Power becomes unconscious and outside a person's awareness.

Too many times, leaders are unaware of the impact of their power. As a result, they are blindsided time and again. These leaders are shocked to find their messages misinterpreted. They do not realize the momentous weight their words carry and are shocked to find that an off-hand remark can create strong negative reactions. Most leaders have no idea how much their power amplifies their message.

> Every time you talk, you are on a **loudspeaker**.
> Your power **amplifies** your message.

With power comes responsibility. Whenever you speak you have an impact. Every word that comes out of your mouth influences people. Each memo, e-mail, and voice mail sends a message. When you least expect it, your words will be repeated, interpreted, and passed along to many others. As with accountable communication, power is energy that must be harnessed and directed.

Symbolic Power versus Real Power

Whether you are a manager, supervisor, CEO, an entrepreneur, a top-level executive, a community leader, a partner in a law firm, a parent, an athletic coach, an informal leader, a celebrity, or the head of a business or staff group, you have power. Having direct reports or a fancy title is inconsequential. Whether you are humble or down-to-earth or come from simple roots is meaningless. If others perceive you as having an impact on their lives, then you have power. The question is *Do you have symbolic power or real power?*

To understand power, we need to begin with what real power is not. Real power is not a title, it is not a position, and it is not money.

Real power is not the number of direct reports, it is not a large office, it is not reporting to the CEO, nor is it having a large budget. Real power is not being in charge of a substantial operational unit nor is it name recognition or celebrity status. These are all symbols of authority: Signs that are used to designate those in charge.

Some symbols of power can be spotted immediately, such as the uniforms of police officers, firefighters, military personnel, or nurses. Some symbols of power are not so obvious, yet these people still have "positions of command," such as parents, teachers, and church leaders. Others have a symbolic power that comes from being in the spotlight, such as celebrities, actors, television stars, sports figures, rock stars, and, once in a while, authors. In business, power is frequently held by titled positions such as members of the Board, the CEO, the COO, the CFO, the senior leadership team, managers, and supervisors.

Even the proximity to authority garners symbolic power. For instance, if a CEO uses an outside consultant as part of his or her inner circle, the consultant is given power. An assistant working closely with a leader, whether administrative or specialized, is often perceived as having authority. It is a grave mistake to underestimate the clout of an assistant. This relationship often involves daily, intimate exchanges of not only information but also observations and subjective judgments. The opinion of an assistant can carry more weight than that of peers or direct reports.

Symbols of power are often mistaken for real power, but they are not the same. Have you ever met an individual with many symbols of power who had little influence over others? I worked with a COO who had all the apparent symbols of power: title, large office, and authority. He also reported to the CEO and was frequently invited to Board meetings. Unfortunately, he had absolutely no power or influence. He was not perceived as powerful, just a figurehead, a "yes" person to the CEO. People listened and responded because they had to, not because they were aligned. In the hallways, they made fun of him and laughed at his attempts to run meetings and provide direction. His symbols of authority made no difference because people did not give him power.

How about the reverse situation? Have you ever met a person who had few traditional symbols of power, but wielded tremendous influence? At the same company as the COO mentioned above, there was an informal leader, an individual contributor with a technical title. The company was in the midst of a cultural change effort, and she took up the mantle for building a high-performance culture. She was recognized for her commitment, accountability, and ability to partner with others. Her credibility and informal leadership continued to grow. People listened to what she said; they were energized by her enthusiasm. She was even invited to senior management meetings to provide input. She had tremendous power—real power not symbolic power.

> ## Perception Is Reality
> *If people believe you have power, you do.*
> *If they think you're an impostor, they're right.*

Power is *not* something you have: It is something others *give* to you. You cannot have power unless others grant it to you. Power does not exist in a vacuum. There are no leaders without followers, just as there are no captains without troops. Power is the relationship between the one who has the power and those who acknowledge it.

Real power is bestowed or granted by others. People give power by believing that that person has the ability to influence, control, or strongly affect their lives. When they believe this, they give the other person power. When they stop believing this, the power disappears.

In the opening of this chapter, the ship's captain assumed he had power over what he believed to be another ship. His assumptions and arrogance were revealed during the exchange of messages. After all he was the captain, the one in charge, the one who gave orders, the one that everyone looked to for direction. To him, it was logical that he gave orders and others quickly complied. The seaman in charge of the lighthouse did not recognize the power of the captain as supreme. Without this recognition, the captain had no power.

The belief people have in your ability to lead, to take care of them, and to provide superior direction is what gives you power, not the symbols of authority. Power is the result of the gifts of trust, loyalty, and support that others *choose* to give you. Whether you believe you are powerful or not is immaterial. When your leadership inspires people, they give you discretionary effort. When they *choose* to let you lead, they grant you power. When people feel safe with you, they give you the gift of trust. If you violate these gifts or take them for granted, you lose credibility and your ability to influence others.

> Position and title do not
> come with automatic rights.
> *Real* power is the **gift** of trust and alignment
> that others **choose** to give to you.

It is not enough to have power; leaders must transform symbolic authority into real power. Spending years stumbling through one communication problem after another is frustrating and unproductive. A new way of thinking is required. Today, power comes from people and relationships. The traditional hierarchical model of status and command rights has been replaced by the new power source of relationships. Once you understand the difference between symbols of authority and real power, this becomes clear. These new insights underscore the need for leaders to gain trust and create authentic alignment.

SYMBOLIC POWER

What you get . . .

- **Minimal effort** to get the job done with spurts of discretionary effort.

- **Resignation and shrinking the game** to defined areas of responsibility.

- **Compliance**—publicly supporting your leadership and initiatives while privately engaging in hallway conspiracies.

- **"Wait and see"** attitude, low-risk and noncommittal behavior.

REAL POWER

What you earn . . .

- **Discretionary effort** above and beyond what is necessary and expected.

- **Ownership, collaboration, and personal accountability** for overall results.

- **Alignment**—authentically supporting your leadership and initiatives in all situations.

- **Trust** and the willingness to make a leap of faith.

Leaders who know how to connect with people and gain their trust are able to tap the collective intelligence and energy of an organization. Power used effectively inspires positive action in others. Used ineffectively, it creates resignation. In a position of authority, you are accountable for your impact on others. Learning how to gain real power to nurture and restore the spirit of people will allow you to produce unprecedented results. It starts with learning the new language of inclusion and cooperation and letting go of the old language of directives and commands.

Living in a Fishbowl

To those who have it, power is not obvious. It is something that simply exists. You probably don't think about power at all—it's automatic. Accepting responsibility and making things happen is what you do every day no matter where you are. Your take-charge attitude and assertive personality naturally move you into positions of authority and status. You are not afraid to take risks, challenge the status quo, and go where no one has gone before. This is what you do, and you are good at it.

But consider how you got to where you are. Even though you are in a position of authority right now, it hasn't always been that way. You grew into this position—you did not just arrive there. But to others you have always had power. Many people did not see your rise up. They just see where you are now. Despite your attempts to convince them that you are just like them, they have a different perspective. To them you came, you arrived, and you have power.

From your viewpoint, there has been a logical progression to your development as a leader. You are the same person you have always been. Position, authority, and status have not changed who you are.

Your core values have remained the same, your beliefs have not altered, and your personality has not changed. You are just doing what you do best—making things happen. In your mind, you think you are like everyone else—just one of the gang working hard to produce results.

But you are not like everyone else. As a leader you are judged by different standards, and no one has ever told you what those standards are. You live in a fishbowl where others watch and judge you at all times. Walk out of a meeting and talk to people in an abrupt manner, and conclusions are immediately drawn. People decide whether you are in a good or bad mood. Their conclusion, accurate or inaccurate, is passed on to others affecting focus, productivity, and morale. Let's face it, you are not one of the gang and never will be again. Until you come to grips with this certainty you will be frustrated, disappointed, and dissatisfied.

> You are **not** one of the gang
> and you never will be again.
> *You live in a fishbowl.*
> *You are being watched at all times.*

In effect, no amount of hard work or visionary ability will make your dreams a reality until you learn how to achieve real power. The only way out of this maze is to understand and be accountable for how your power impacts others.

Seriously Underestimating Your Power

Because you are a leader, what you say is put on "loudspeaker" and magnified many times. Your words blast through an organization at the speed of light. How you say something is dissected, examined, and scrutinized at the most detailed level. You are in the spotlight and nothing you say or do will take you out of it.

> *Problems occur not because leaders **have** power but because they **behave** as if they don't.*

From your point of view, communication should be easy. When you say "go left," that's what you mean: Go left. But that is *not* what they hear. Your power, position, and authority color everything. You think you are saying the right thing, using the right words, and then Wham! Suddenly and inexplicably you are in trouble. Someone reacts to what you said or did not say, how you said it, the words you used, or the images your words created. Whatever you said is gone from your mind. Although you have moved on, others have not. They are replaying your words over and over again in their minds. Worse yet they are spreading the word and telling others what you "said," and it isn't good. And it *is* true that bad news travels fast—very, very fast.

You now have a dilemma. As a leader, your job is to create a compelling future and bring new realities into existence. Yet how you speak often leaves people immobilized and locked in the past. They are stuck with words you wish you never said—words that damage people's spirits. Instead of inspiring people, your words can paralyze them and stop the action.

Producing results would be easy if you weren't working with people. But that would require that you live on another planet. Your job is to produce results through people, not in spite of them. To achieve real power, there are three undeniable truths that leaders must understand:

1. You have power.

2. You underestimate your power.

3. You are not in control of your power.

The last statement is the most difficult to accept. The sooner you realize you are not in control, the faster you can get out of your own way. How others perceive and experience you determines your future. You can influence and shape your future, but you cannot control people. Try it and you will fail. This is one reality you cannot escape unless you work alone, report to no one, and retreat to your cave at the end of each day.

The Invisible Cloak: How You Wear Power

There are three typical ways in which leaders don the cloak of power: They reduce power, amplify power, or respect power. How do you respond to having power? You may vacillate between two response styles or find you have a definite preference.

Response 1: Leaders Who Reduce Power

Talking as if they are one of the gang. Minimizing or reducing power by using an overabundance of deferring statements, hedges, and softeners.

Response 2: Leaders Who Amplify Power

Using exclusive language, directives, commands, and parental language when speaking. Talking and speaking with little or no awareness of their impact on others.

Response 3: Leaders Who Respect Power

Being accountable for their impact on others—the source of *real power*, not symbolic authority. Speaking to connect with people and gain their trust by using the language of inclusion and cooperation.

The first response, the denial of power, is fueled by the need to be liked and accepted. Frequently, this response occurs with people new to leadership positions who find it awkward to take charge, especially if they are managing someone who was previously their peer or boss. To downplay their newly acquired position and demonstrate to others that they have not changed, they often defer decisions to others, allowing consensus to dominate decision-making. Although a fine leadership skill, consensus used to the exclusion of taking a stand and making unpopular decisions erodes both the credibility and results of leaders.

Avoiding Making Decisions
Speaking That Derails

- "It's your decision. I'm just here to provide information."

- "What do you think? I'll just go along with the group."

- "Whatever you decide is fine with me. I'm just here to support you."

- "I'd rather not decide. It's up to the team."

Why it doesn't work: Using questions exclusively minimizes power and defers decision making to others. On the surface, this looks good. The problem is that the leader avoids taking unpopular stands. The word *just* in this context says, "I'm not important here." It diminishes the value of the person speaking and reduces power.

Those who love power tend to use directives and exclusionary and parental language. This type of speaking can unconsciously trigger emotional reactions of defiance. Since the earliest association with power is by and large the parent-child relationship, it is understandable why people revert to language learned in the home. Parental, directive language is appropriate and necessary for the safety and well-being of children. As a child grows into an adult, this language is typically replaced with words that provide choice rather than command statements.

Speaking in a commanding "I want, I need, I will have" manner turns people off. Let's take the example of the leader who says, "You should know what to do. I've told you what I want more than once!" This type of message shuts people down and causes them to clam up. Adults do not like being told what they should and should not do. One of the most pressing problems revealed in employee surveys is that people do not feel safe to speak up. When managers and leaders send a message telling others their input is not needed or valued, people become resigned and shrink the game. Say good-bye to discretionary effort.

Shutting People Down
Speaking That Derails

- "I've made my decision. Now let's move on."

- "I want this handled immediately and this is what I want done. . . ."

- "I will not tolerate this. Change it now."

- "You've got to be kidding! This is not what I asked for."

Why it doesn't work: The predominance of the word *I* (instead of *we*, *our*, or *us*) is an example of exclusionary language. Leaders who fall in love with power speak as if they are the center of the universe with everyone else revolving around them.

The third and most effective response to having status and authority is a "respect for power." This balanced response is what gives leaders real power rather than symbolic authority. It takes into account how power impacts people. When a leader respects power—rather than minimizing power or resorting to control—people feel included, valued, and personally connected to the leader. People respond by giving trust, experiencing authentic alignment, and acting as owners. Collaborating and working together is fun and easy. Morale goes up as people feel that they are a valued part of the team, group, or organization. Leaders who have a healthy respect for power create an environment of collaboration and trust.

Collaborating and Including People
Speaking Accountably

- "We face a number of challenges such as . . ."

- "We had a tough first quarter but I'm optimistic about what we can do. . . ."

- "We can't ignore the problem but together we can resolve it."

- "We need everyone on board."

Why it works: The use of the word *we* is an example of inclusionary language. People feel connected, included, and valued. They are not alone; they are part of a larger group, and the leader is right in there with them.

Bear in mind that people want to contribute and make a difference. It is up to the leader to foster an environment of cooperation and partnership. The language of inclusion extends to words and phrases that elicit the feeling of being valued and included as part of a winning team.

Collaborating and Working Together
Speaking Accountably

- Our team, our group, our future

- Collaborate

- Cooperate

- Commit to the success of one another

- Work together

- Together

- All of us

- With your support

- Trust the commitment of people

- Partner

- Team player
- Helpful
- Support one another
- Relationships

- Side-by-side
- Unbeatable team
- Collectively
- Join forces

The difference between symbolic power and real power is the common thread that runs through this discussion. Real power is both respecting your power and being accountable for how it affects others. The shift from symbolic authority to real power unlocks the ability of people to be extraordinary leaders.

Compliance Is *Not* Alignment

You cannot use authority, control, or power to manipulate or control people without grave consequences. Leaders who consciously or unconsciously use their power forcefully face serious repercussions. People will comply only to protect their jobs and careers.

But compliance is not alignment. Compliance is a temporary accommodation to meet the requirements of the person in charge. On the surface, compliance appears to be agreement. Below the surface, it frequently erupts into passive-aggressive behavior: people doing and saying things that are in direct contradiction with what you think they agreed to. When people say "yes" to something or someone, they do not authentically agree with, they resent it—big time. Compliance leads to hallway conspiracies, people privately conferring and disagreeing with you while publicly complying with what you want. Compliance is the furthest thing from ownership and accountability. It is temporary, fleeting, and does not represent genuine leadership support.

Alignment, on the other hand, is when people set aside their personal preferences and own the decision or direction as if they were the authors of it. Because alignment is an authentic choice, people talk and behave as owners. There is no blame, finger-pointing, or resentment in their speaking. When leaders use their power as force they get compliance; when leaders are accountable for their use of power they get alignment.

The way in which you speak creates a reaction in others. The most frequent misuse of power is speaking in a parental, "command-and-control" manner. Language that generates alignment acknowledges your authority while simultaneously including others. This language produces authentic alignment where words and behavior are consistent, makes people feel safe to speak up, and inspires people to make things happen.

Phrases that result in compliance are, in effect, control statements. These types of statements shut people down so they do not speak up; produce compliance, a false sense of alignment, and hallway conspiracies; and create negative reactions.

⊐◇⊏

Phrases That Produce Compliance	Phrases That Generate Alignment
Avoid:	**Replace with:**
• Don't question me.	• Ask any question you have: There is no such thing as an

	unimportant question. Your thoughts are valuable to me.
• Do it because I said it.	• My opinion is one point of view. This has to be a decision we make together.
• I'm in charge here, not you.	• Although I have the final responsibility, I sincerely want your input.
• I make the decisions.	• You can always count on me to listen. I may not always agree, but I will always listen.
• You heard me.	• When you do not understand something I say, it means I did not explain it well. So please ask me to clarify whatever is on your mind.

When you have compliance instead of alignment, people give minimum effort and do only what they need to do. A command-and-control leader, one who amplifies power, is viewed as a bully rather than a credible and inspiring leader. Under the reign (or terror) of command and control, morale and performance suffer. Additionally, people do not feel connected with a leader who is exclusionary and directive. The need for an authentic relationship with a leader is strong. People want to feel included, inspired, and connected to their leaders.

Key Communication Principles

Principle 1: You are not one of the gang and never will be again.

Think Twice. People want leaders to lead. You are no longer one of the gang, and they don't want you to be. What people want is for leaders to lead, not win a popularity contest. This means being willing to take a stand, go out on a limb, or take an unpopular position. Trying to be one of the gang minimizes your ability to lead and annoys others. People already know you are not one of the gang. They know that you have power and authority over them. You can be collaborative and be a strong leader without resorting to command-and-control tactics.

Action. If you have a tendency to minimize your power, practice using declarative statements (rather than questions) to express your point of view.

Principle 2: You are the last person to hear about what is really going on.

Think Twice. Once you are a leader, information goes underground. You are the last person to hear what is going on. Hallway conspiracies and the grapevine replace direct communication to you.

Action. Practice giving people explicit permission to ask questions, give you feedback, and coach you. The more you do this, the more you will receive direct communication.

Principle 3: You cannot **not** communicate.

Think Twice. All behavior communicates. You cannot *not* communicate—there is no such thing. No response is a response. Your words, tone of voice, silence, and behavior communicate a message. Everything you do or do not do communicates. You are in a fishbowl, and everyone is watching and judging you.

Action. When communicating, ask yourself: "What message am I really sending?" When in doubt, reconsider what you are communicating.

Principle 4: Real power is what others give you: the gifts of their trust, alignment, and support.

Think Twice. Symbolic power—the symbols of title, authority, and status—are not the same as real power. Real power is what others choose to give you. You cannot have a leader without followers. You get your power from others. They give you the gifts of trust, alignment, and support.

Action. Do one thing each day that allows people to connect with you. This might include encouraging someone, including someone, or asking a person for his or her input. Demonstrate that others are important.

Section II

Your Words and How They Trigger *Action* and *Reaction*

4

The Black Hole

How to Make Your Point So What You Say Is What They Hear

Your Purpose

To maximize understanding and reduce confusion by providing positive direction, clarity, and focus.

The best way to really enter minds that hate complexity and confusion is to oversimplify your message. . . . The lesson here is not to try and tell your entire story. Just focus on one powerful attribute and drive it into the mind.

Jack Trout with Steve Rivkin
The New Positioning

The chairperson of a Fortune 100 company expressed frustration about her senior management team: "We discuss our strategic business issues, then align on strategy. Six months later I discover nothing has been implemented. I'm upset and disappointed. They actually think they are giving me what I want. They're not listening at all! All this time and work and nothing sticks."

This is not a unique frustration or concern for leaders. In over 20 years of working with CEOs and executives, a recurrent theme emerges: *Employees don't do what I say.* The problem exists on both small and large scales. Major organizational initiatives, such as total quality management, reengineering, and high performance, result in little or no action. Or a project report that was due on your desk Monday morning is still not there by Thursday.

But my communication is clear and direct, you argue. It may be in your mind but not to others. You think you send clear messages. Then you are blindsided by a complete and utter misunderstanding of what you think you said. Perhaps it is a report, a review of project results, or something as simple as distributing a memo to a select group. You stare in disbelief at the documents and/or people in front of you. How in the world did they come up with this after you were explicit and spoke directly to the point? You feel enormously let down and aggravated with their incompetence.

Stop and listen carefully: What you said is not what they heard. Communication is fraught with difficulties because we think our words carry the same meaning for others as they do for us. They do not. Words are symbolic, and people attach their own private interpretation to what you say. For example, a disgruntled leader walked into a meeting with his direct reports. He told them in no uncertain terms they were failing miserably in demonstrating their commitment to the high-performance initiative, and he wanted this situation corrected fast. The leader envisioned his direct reports setting up discussions and meetings where they could talk face-to-face with their subordinates. But his direct reports had a different interpretation. They moved fast, sending memos and e-mails to their subordinates. Same words—different meaning.

When a leader fails to clearly communicate his or her expectations, problems occur. Unmet expectations lead to disappointments—lots of them. People filter and interpret what they think you mean and do what they think you want. The operational word is *think*. Without clarity, focus, and direction, the probability of accurate message transmission is low.

There is a great distance between what you say and what they hear. Bridging this distance to ensure controlled meaning and understanding of your messages is the purpose of this chapter.

Entering the Black Hole

What causes the gap between *your* direction and *their* implementation and execution? To answer this question, let's begin with where your messages are sent. They travel to the black hole: the place in the mind where all messages end up for interpreting, sorting, storing, or deleting. Noise and competing stimuli are coming from all directions. Your message journeys into minds that are inundated and overwhelmed with too much information, changes, confusion, and uncertainty. Every time you speak, numerous factors affect how your words are interpreted and acted upon. It is not surprising that messages become scrambled or lost altogether.

How can you maximize understanding and reduce confusion? Numerous outside forces affect what people hear, but there is only one force you can control: you. Focusing on changing others does not solve the problem. In fact, this *is* the problem—you're thinking it is they and not you. Sometimes it is they, and you are dealing with a competency issue. However, you must carefully discern if the failure to execute is a competency or communication issue. A competency issue tells you the person is in the wrong job. A communication issue reveals the need for greater clarity and precision. Organizations lose many talented people by incorrectly diagnosing this important distinction.

Let's return to the chairperson in the example at the opening of this chapter. To produce a different outcome, she could (1) hire new people, (2) change the behavior of others, or (3) change what she is doing. It takes more time, money, and effort to attempt to alter the behavior of people. Plus the success ratio is quite low when it comes to changing others. Short of designing a customized program to teach people how to understand you, the most expedient route is to work on how you can say it right the first time. Not only will it prevent countless breakdowns but it will also put you in the driver's seat. Instead of expecting or hoping that others will understand, you can steer the conversation in the direction *you* want it to go.

It starts with having the right focus. A great deal of time is wasted when leaders travel down the ineffective path of trying to change others. When it comes to getting your point across, you must first ask yourself, "Where is my focus?"

Where Is Your Focus?

Question 1: How can I get others to *listen* better? *Or*

Question 2: How can I *say* what I want them to hear?

The first question, "How can I get others to listen better?" focuses on changing how others hear and process information. Although the question seems to ask, "What can I do?" it actually places accountability on what other people do or do not do. The question implies that others are responsible for how they listen. Of course it is true: People *are* responsible for how they listen, but that is a subject for another book. The focus of this book is how to alter the way in which you communicate to dramatically increase results. The second question emphasizes your accountability and places full emphasis on what you say. Once again, you are in control. You can always change your own behavior. Always.

What You Said Is Not What They Heard

People cannot do what you say until they understand what you want. The problem with communication is that we use words and phrases without recognizing that they mean different things to different people. When you say, "I want more effort," what do people hear? Most likely they hear your disappointment in them. When private meanings are assigned to shared words, the result is confusion, anxiety, and chaos. What comes out of your mouth journeys a long way before it is interpreted, filtered, massaged, and finally heard.

JUST BECAUSE YOU *"SAID IT"* DOES *NOT* MEAN . . .

Anyone heard you.
Anyone heard you correctly.
Anyone cares.

Have you ever seen what happens when someone says, "I don't understand"? A typical response of the speaker is to talk louder and repeat the message using the exact same words. Increasing volume or duplicating a message does not magically make people understand. Instead, it annoys them. When people say, "I don't understand," they are asking for clarification, not repetition with volume. Do not confuse using the same words with the need to repeat your message using multiple communication channels (for example, electronic, verbal, or written). The key to understanding and retention is to deliver the same message or theme in *different* ways.

JUST BECAUSE YOU SAID IT *REPEATEDLY* DOES *NOT* MEAN . . .

Anyone is moving.
Anyone is moving fast.
Anyone is moving in the right direction.

How a leader communicates expectations makes all the difference. A message about working harder, for example, can create an uproar in an organization when words are misunderstood. In one company, the head of a business unit, in a moment of frustration, said she did not want to see the parking lot empty at 5 p.m. She was making a point, not being literal. But too late. Her words created a reaction. What the employees heard was, "No matter when you arrive, you are not to leave until well after 5 p.m." Quite a few employees usually arrived early to work, starting at 6 a.m. when the office was quiet, and they could accomplish a great deal. After hearing the leader's message, they changed their behavior all right. They stayed until after 5 p.m. but no longer came early to work. By expressing her frustration in an unclear manner, the leader lost what she was trying to gain: greater productivity and efficiency.

WHAT YOU SAY and WHAT THEY HEAR

What *You* Say: We have an exciting new opportunity.
What *They* Hear: We have a lot more work.

What *You* Say: This new initiative focuses on our quality efforts.
What *They* Hear: This new initiative focuses on blah, blah, blah.

What *You* Say: This is urgent; it is our top priority.
What *They* Hear: Everything is urgent.

What *You* Say:	I need to see harder work, more effort, and better results.
What *They* Hear:	Give me your firstborn.
What *You* Say:	We have a major organizational change.
What *They* Hear:	Start looking for another job.

So why is it so difficult for people to understand what you are saying? Why is your message often misinterpreted? How can people possibly be confused after you have delivered a clear, straightforward statement? How can one word or phrase spoken by you create so much commotion? How many times do you have to repeat the same message for people to get it? Why is communication such a challenge?

The reason: We are not speaking the same language. Just because we use the same verbal communication system within a culture does not mean we are speaking the same language. It is as if one person is speaking Spanish and the other French. People have their own unique filter for interpreting what they hear and supplying what's missing. They filter what you say through colored lenses based on the past, their personal history, preferences, and many other areas. For instance, when people are resigned and skeptical, they hear a version of "here we go again" every time you speak. Leaders are deluded into believing that everyone speaks the same language and therefore has the same meanings for words.

The Mind Fills in the Blanks

If your message is unclear or ambiguous, others will fill in the blanks by making up the meaning in their minds. People filter what you say based on their personal experiences and beliefs. Your words are translated and interpreted. The mind makes meaning out of information by building patterns, filling in the blanks, and selectively attending to information and stimuli. If a manager, for instance, has a high regard for an employee, he or she will adjust all information to support this view. The "anointed chosen ones" can do no wrong regardless of information to the contrary. Similarly when people "fall in love," they only hear and attend to information that supports their beliefs. The rest is discarded. When the feeling of "falling in love" is replaced with "being in love," the lost illusion is often enough to destroy a budding relationship.

The following story offers a good example of how the mind selectively attends to information and then fills in the blanks to support the existing beliefs.

There was a well-liked farmer who was accused of stealing a pig from a rancher who was disliked by everyone. They went to court over the pig, and the jurors rendered the following verdict: *"The farmer is not guilty, **but he must return the pig.**"*

The judge was perplexed by this verdict. He instructed the jurors to leave and not return until they had a verdict that made sense. The jurors left the room, and their loud voices could be heard down the hall. Shortly they returned and the judge asked, "Have you reached a new verdict?" "We have, your honor," answered the foreman. *"The farmer is not guilty, **and he can keep the pig.**"*

The moral to the story is clear: People will find evidence or distort information and reality to fit their beliefs. Or said another way, meanings are in people, not in words. The question remains: Why do people fill in the blanks? Because they want certainty, meaning, and purpose. People want to know they are on the right track and that what they are doing supports the larger efforts of the organization. The mind filters and interprets every message it receives. When the message is unclear, ambiguous, or incomplete, the mind fills in the blanks.

Communicating to Both Minds

There is hope. You can maximize understanding and reduce confusion by communicating to two minds, not one. To inspire positive action, both the conscious and unconscious mind must be engaged. If you want your message to be understood, talk to the conscious mind (left brain); if you want it to be remembered, communicate to the unconscious mind (right brain).

The conscious mind wants structure and order whereas the unconscious mind remembers feelings and subjective experiences. Further, the conscious mind has limited storage capacity, which explains why people can easily forget information especially when there is a lot of it. In contrast, the unconscious mind has unlimited memory and storage capacity. This clarifies why people can remember feelings and experiences but forget what was said. It is essential to leave people with positive experiences because when everything else fades, they still remember how you made them feel.

> *Long after people forget what you said,*
> *they remember how you made them feel.*

Most leaders do not understand the difference between the two minds. Their information-loaded messages often miss the mark as they present facts, logic, and details to the conscious mind while ignoring the subjective feelings and experiences recorded by the unconscious. The consequence? People are unenthused; while you are speaking they're thinking, "Here we go again."

When you communicate accountably, you engage both the conscious and unconscious minds and inspire positive action. Let's examine how this works. The words *inspiration* and *positive* fit into the category of feelings or subjective experiences. How people feel when they walk away from a discussion or meeting is stored in the unconscious. This includes feelings such as inspired, deflated, upset, angry, encouraged, or demoralized. Long after people forget what you said, they remember how you made them feel.

The word *action* connotes moving forward in a specific direction and falls in the category of logic and thinking, the domain of the conscious mind. People structure and organize what you say and fill in the blanks where information is missing. This takes place in the conscious mind. If you fail to clarify the outcome for a sensitive discussion, for example, the listener will search for your agenda rather than attending to the message.

What happens when you communicate exclusively to one side of the brain? If you communicate only to the conscious mind, you may get your point across, but in the end there will be little enthusiasm and only intellectual buy-in. On the other hand, when you communicate only to the unconscious mind, people experience positive feelings and are inspired, but there is no action.

The short version is that the conscious mind needs structure and order; the unconscious records feelings and experiences. When you don't provide structure and order, people fill in the blanks. When you fail to provide positive experiences, people withhold their energy and commitment. The mission is to communicate to the two minds. Maximize understanding, reduce confusion, and ensure retention by providing organization for the conscious mind, and creating positive experiences for the unconscious.

Give the Conscious Mind STRUCTURE AND ORDER	Give the Unconscious Mind POSITIVE EXPERIENCES
• **Say what you want:** Be clear and concise. Keep it simple and straightforward. **Example:** *I want you to champion this initiative.*	• **Focus on positive outcomes:** State your outcome in positive language. Be specific. **Example:** *Our outcome is to align on how to introduce the initiative.*
• **Emphasize what is important:** Highlight critical messages and key points. Focus on only one or two. Keep it bite-size. **Example:** *There are two specific areas that need your attention.*	• **Talk in positive language:** Reinforce what you want (e.g., "improve productivity" versus "avoid inefficiency"). **Example:** *Our first task is to enroll and engage others.*
• **Be specific about expectations:** Clearly	• **Create positive feelings:** Express how you value the

communicate what you want and include a "by when" time frame.
Example: *I want a written plan by Tuesday.*

person and the relationship.

Example: *Your leadership makes a tremendous difference. I appreciate your energy and commitment.*

Why it works: When you provide order and structure for the conscious mind, people listen to what you are saying, rather than search for your agenda.

Why it works: When you provide an encouraging focus and leave people with positive feelings, it raises spirits and morale. People want to feel good.

Solving the Right Problem

One of the most common communication breakdowns is trying to solve a problem before understanding it. That's why discussing desired outcomes before the discussion gets under way is invaluable. The mere act of mutually agreeing on the outcome or problem forces critical thinking and analysis. A lot of time is wasted when people are solving different problems or the wrong problem.

Outcomes provide direction for the conscious mind. When you start a discussion or meeting, tell people what you want or ask everyone to mutually agree on the outcome. If you don't, they will fill in the blanks or stop listening altogether. Keep in mind that when the conscious mind has insufficient direction and focus, it wanders. The purpose of starting with your outcome is to orient participants in the discussion. It also allows the conscious mind to stop searching for the agenda. In turn, people relax and message receptivity increases.

Discuss Outcomes *Before* Solutions
Speaking Accountably

- "Now, before we jump to solving this problem, let's both agree on where we are headed."

- "Let's make sure we are solving the same problem. What do you see as the issue?"

- "What results do we want from our meeting today?"

- "What problem are we trying to solve?"

- "I want to defer discussing any solutions until we have a complete understanding of the problem. Now, what happened . . . ?"

Why it works: The conscious mind works best with structure and direction. When you start with your outcome, you define where the conversation is headed. Conversely, having no outcome or solving the wrong problem produces uncertainty and confusion and wastes time. The above statements rein in the discussion so solutions are not the issue until the problem is correctly identified.

Once the outcome or desired results are mutually agreed upon, then generating solutions makes sense. As you engage in the conversation, periodically check to make sure all parties are focused on the same outcome or problem. This is exceptionally useful in meetings where conversations have a way of wandering off to topics unrelated to solving the problem.

Communicating Priorities

People cannot read your mind. If you have a preference for how and when something is to be done, say it; do not imply it. Otherwise, you will be disappointed when your employees do not deliver what you want. Managers frequently assume people know what to do and then are disappointed with the results. To avoid disappointment, clearly articulate your expectations.

> **Do not be disappointed**
> when people don't give you what you didn't ask for.

There are only two conditions when it is acceptable not to set priorities: (1) You do not have a preference for when or how a project is handled, or (2) you have given the other party accountability for making these decisions. As a word of caution, even the best performers will make judgment calls different from yours. So when you give people accountability, do not crucify them when they do not do what you would have done. Great minds do not always think alike.

Your choice is to state clearly expectations and priorities or to give people accountability to make these decisions. Doing something in between, such as implying expectations or talking in generalities, only serves to increase anxiety and stress. It naturally follows that when stress and anxiety are on the rise, performance and productivity go down.

✦

When Priorities Are Unclear

Speaking That Derails

- "This needs to be done by Friday along with everything else."

- "Just add this to your list."

- "This is important. But don't forget about . . ."

- "You set the priorities, just make sure you get 'X,' 'Y,' and 'Z' done also."

- "I want this done as soon as possible."

- "I'd like to see the results this week."

- "Make this your top priority along with 'X,' 'Y,' and 'Z.'"

Why it doesn't work: The statements are vague and ambiguous. Additionally, some statements create confusion and send an incongruent message such as, "Put this at the top of your list along with 'X,' 'Y,' and 'Z.'" Now *everything* is at the top of the list, and all order has been eliminated. Priorities remain unclear and unresolved.

Be explicit when you give people accountability. Do not assume anything. Make sure others understand the extent of their accountability or two weeks later they will be knocking at your door to ask you a question that you expected them to answer.

Giving Others Responsibility
Speaking Accountably

- "You know what's on your plate. Let me know by Friday what is a reasonable deadline for you."

- "Think about how quickly this can be done without sacrificing other critical areas. Can you tell me Monday when this can be completed?"

- "This is a priority assignment. How and when can you accomplish this? Think about it and advise me early next week."

Why it works: The statements are direct; each has a specific action requested. The individual is asked to look at the big picture and establish priorities and a time for completion. Asking for a "by when" time makes the request manageable. It gives you something tangible—a time commitment for holding the person accountable for delivery.

In business today there are many competing priorities. When you add one more to the pile, order and urgency must be determined. If you do not communicate priorities, others will establish them. In many cases this is exactly what you expect of people reporting to you: the ability to establish priorities. However, this still requires a mutual understanding of what is urgent and what is *really* urgent. Basically, information is sorted into these two categories. Everything competes for top billing. Being clear about your expectations requires discipline on your part. It means knowing precisely what you want and stating it clearly.

> If everything is urgent, nothing is urgent.
> An **"everything must be done now"** message
> cancels out both order and speed.

Checking Clarity and Assumptions along the Way

Reviewing along the way what people are hearing is a useful and efficient skill. If you wait until the end of a lengthy discussion or meeting, you will have wasted valuable time. Checking for clarity during a conversation helps you avoid surprises. Your purpose is to review where you are in the discussion and verify assumptions and clarify meaning.

Checking for Clarity

Speaking Accountably

- "Before we move on to the next point, let me see if I understand you clearly . . ."

- "I want to make sure I understand where we both are in this discussion. Are you saying . . . ?"

- "Let's pause for a second and see if we both agree on . . ."

- "Before going any further, here's what I see as the challenge. . . . Does this match your understanding?"

Why it works: Problem solving and decisions are based on cumulative premises and assertions. The above statements provide a way to press the pause button and check for mutual understanding.

Checking for clarity also includes examining assumptions. It is not news that assumptions can get people in trouble. Because meanings are in people, not in words, it is important to discover how people interpret what you are saying. Stop the discussion and ask for clarification of specific statements or vague words.

Checking Assumptions
Speaking Accountably

- "When you say 'X,' what do you mean?"

- "When I said 'X,' I meant . . . Is that what you heard?"

- "I assumed that meant . . . Is this true for you?"

- "Is that your experience?"

- "Is this your understanding?"

Why it works: The questions gather information about how the individual interpreted a message. Since all messages are filtered, it is essential to find out what the person really heard. If you do not check assumptions along the way, you will not discover the difference in interpretation until a breakdown occurs. This often results in costly mistakes and lost time.

Tell Them What You Want, Not What You Don't Want

One of the most common pitfalls for leaders is focusing on what is inconsistent, missing, wrong, or inaccurate. Trained in critical thinking and analysis, leaders often attend to what is missing before they communicate what is needed. As a result, many leaders are more highly skilled in articulating what they don't want than what they do want.

How about you? Are the first words out of your mouth centered on what is wrong? If your answer is "yes," you belong to an ever-expanding group. Hectic schedules, stress, and the need to get things done fast exacerbate this situation. Correcting, fixing, or avoiding takes precedence over creating, building, or generating. This approach would be fine if negative input and direction (that is, what is *not* wanted or needed) motivated people. It seldom does. In the short term, negative direction can light a fire and get people to take action. In the long term, feeling valued and appreciated diminishes, along with meaning and purpose, and morale falls.

The problem is not that leaders use negative or "what's missing" statements. The problem is talking only in negatives or ignoring the order in which issues are presented. Start with a positive outcome before discussing what needs to be corrected.

The unconscious mind stores and remembers how things feel. When you are unhappy with the performance of someone who reports to you, how do you communicate? Do you start with "I'm not getting good feedback on your . . ." This start typifies the "what's missing" approach. The person hears, "Don't do this, don't do that." Telling a person what's missing is generally based on a breakdown or problem. It is easy to articulate what happened and what needs to be corrected. It is much more difficult, but infinitely more powerful, to generate and articulate the future you want for someone.

Provide Positive Direction
Speaking Accountably

- **Avoid:** "I'm not getting good feedback on how your group is partnering with others."

Replace with: "I want you to lead the way in building a collaborative organization known for its partnerships with other business units. To do this, we need to work together on . . ."

- **Avoid:** "Your people are not responding well to your leadership. They do not feel that you listen."

Replace with: "I need your help in raising morale. Specifically, I want you to create a safe environment where people feel heard and valued. This means that we need to take a look at the feedback from your people on . . ."

- **Avoid:** "You miss important details in your analysis and reports."

Replace with: "You and I are both committed to quality. I need you to model and demonstrate quality in everything you do. To start with, we need to . . ."

Why it works: Unless you are ready to fire the individual, paint a positive picture of what you want. When you provide positive direction, inspiration, and a clear focus on what is needed, the response is immediate and favorable. Negative direction can also get an immediate response, but it is usually not favorable.

Positive statements yield positive results. When you focus people on what you want, they head in that direction. If you only tell people what you don't want, they lose focus and inspiration. The key is to balance how you communicate. Of course it is necessary to communicate what's missing and wrong. However, if done in a positive framework, people will be more efficient and effective in correcting the problem. The best formula is to "frame" your message so that what you want is the goal and correcting what's missing is the way to achieve it.

Delivering Negative Feedback in a Positive Way
Speaking Accountably

Step 1: Provide positive direction

You: "The reason I wanted to meet is to make sure we are both heading in the same direction."

Why it works: Starting with a positive outcome sets the tone for the conversation. It also establishes a feeling of partnership. Starting with negative direction, such as, "Your recent report was full of mistakes," leaves the person feeling alone and on the defensive.

Step 2: State your concern

You: "Your recent report raised some questions for me. I'd like to go over several specific points."

Why it works: "Being direct works. People respond well to a straightforward comment."

Step 3: Take accountability

SUBORDINATE: "I wasn't sure what you wanted and hopefully this discussion will help me."

YOU: "That's my intention. I want to make sure I'm clear about what is needed from you."

Why it works: Accountable language is non-blameful. The statement "I want to make sure I'm clear . . ." is an example of taking accountability and using the word *I* instead of *you*. On the other hand, if you said, "You need to be clear . . . ," this statement places responsibility on the other party, points the finger, and damages the relationship.

Marking Out Key Points

You already know that the mind wanders, and people do not listen to every word you say. Auditory and visual distractions, competing information, and other interruptions vie for attention. The mind treats all this information equally unless the critical message is marked out or highlighted. In verbal communication, we do this with voice intonation, inflection, and body language. In written messages, we use different fonts, layouts, or print techniques. In conversations, we can use sentence starters, which are phrases at the beginning of a sentence that allow the mind to transition to what you are about to say and remember and mark out your critical points.

The mind takes in an enormous amount of information but what gets saved and stored depends a great deal on how you say it. Because the mind wanders in and out, sentence starters—specific words at the beginning of a sentence—cue the listener about the importance of what is coming next. Without starters the mind does not have time to transition. Additionally, when everything is presented as having the same importance, the mind of the listener chooses when to check in and check out. You don't get to choose. Nobody attends 100 percent to a conversation, meeting, or presentation.

It only takes a second or two for the mind to adjust and listen in a directed way. Sentence starters provide structure and direction for the conscious mind. While you are talking to people, they are trying to make sense out of what you are saying. Then halfway through your message, they understand. But in the process, they missed half of what you said.

Marking out or highlighting your key points, theme, requests, or message is invaluable. In the absence of marking out crucial points, the mind will either treat everything as equal or "make up" what is important. It is a lot easier to be clear on the front end about what you want than to engage in rework on the back end because others did not understand.

✦

Marking Out Key Points
Speaking Accountably

- "The key point is . . ."

- "The key feature is . . ."

- "What is most important to recognize is . . ."

- "The real challenge is . . ."

- "We have only one focus. It is . . ."

- "You should anticipate one critical change . . ."

- "If you remember one point, remember this . . ."

- "Here is the most important thing for you to remember . . ."

- "Listen carefully to what I am about to say."

- "The next thing I am going to say will surprise you, but it is my main point . . ."

- "Of everything I have said to you, there are two things I want you to act on."

Why it works: When you mark out or highlight key statements, people remember them. The mind does not stay focused all the time; it wanders. When introducing or stating your primary or key point, use a sentence starter to give the mind time to transition and refocus.

A word of caution: If you overuse sentence starters, you will be treating everything with the same level of importance. If everything is critical, nothing is critical. Pick and choose when to use sentence starters. More is not better.

Focus Attention on the Critical Message
Speaking Accountably

PEER: "We have several options. We can make a decision today or take our chances and wait. What are your thoughts?"

YOU: "That's true, we could wait, but there is one thing that stands out for me (pause): Our competitors are already moving on this."

Why it works: The key point is presented with a sentence starter: "There is one thing that stands out for me." The mind notes it is about to hear critical information. When you add a starter, you verbally underline the important facts.

Bringing It All Together

The problem with summarizing is that you do it. Stop. Do not summarize what you have said. Ask others to do this. How else are you going to determine if you both have the same meaning? Falling into the trap of repeating your main points in a summary is just another opportunity for the mind to wander.

Ask Others to Summarize Your Message
Speaking Accountably

- "Would you take a moment and summarize our actions?"

- "Help me make sure I've been clear. What are the key points you heard?"

- "What main points stand out for you in the discussion we've just had?"

- "What message are you walking away with today?"

- "I've been talking too much. Would you summarize our agreements and next steps?"

- "Let's see if I've communicated well. How about summarizing our actions."

- "Let's check my thinking. What are the key points? Have I missed anything?"

Why it works: By asking others to summarize, you make them an active, rather than passive, participant in the conversation. Being active increases the likelihood for positive impact and retention. Additionally, it allows you to listen and make sure that what you said is what they heard.

When the situation does not allow for others to summarize, by all means, summarize your key points. By using sentence starters, you cue the mind to listen for the important message in your discussion or presentation.

Summarizing Your Own Message
Speaking Accountably

- "What all this means is . . ."

- "Taken together, what I am saying is . . ."

- "Ultimately . . ."

- "Finally . . ."

- "In short . . ."

- "My message is . . ."

- "In effect . . ."

- "Collectively . . ."

Why it works: By using a brief phrase immediately prior to your summary, people know they are about to hear important information. This provides the mind with structure, organization, and direction.

You may be in a meeting with your boss or a peer. Perhaps his or her real message or key points is not clear. This is a place where you can intervene during the discussion to assist in marking out the primary message.

Summarizing Another's Message
Speaking Accountably

- "One theme you keep coming back to seems to be . . ."

- "Let's review what we've discussed so far."

- "I've been thinking about what you've said. I see something that I'd like to ask about. Did you mean . . . ?"

- "As I've been listening to you, your main concern seems to be . . ."

- "Let's recap what we've said so far."

Why it works: When you summarize another's message, you not only demonstrate you are carefully listening but you also assist the individual in articulating his or her key message. Most people appreciate an active discussion partner who helps them process information out loud.

Key Communication Principles

Principle 1: What you said is not what they heard.

Think Twice. All messages are filtered and interpreted. The mind fades in and out when listening to another person. Providing clear, direct, and positive messages helps the mind focus and retain what you communicate. In the absence of this, the mind will fill in the blanks and make up its own meaning.

Action. Practice stating your outcome or mutually agreeing on the problem and/or challenge before you begin the discussion. This will get you in the habit of communicating what you want on the front end of discussions.

Principle 2: Long after people forget what you said, they remember how you made them feel.

Think Twice. People remember experiences and feelings more accurately than they recall words. Positive outcomes and direction foster an environment where even the most difficult conversations can leave people feeling good.

Action. Ask people how they feel at the end of the conversation. Simply ask, "How do you feel about our discussion? Have I left you feeling positive and inspired or have I missed something?" This gives people an opportunity to reflect on how they are feeling, and it gives you a chance to correct anything that is missing.

Principle 3: When everything is urgent, nothing is urgent.

Think Twice. The mind treats all information as equal unless important points are highlighted or marked out. When leaders fall into the trap of "wanting everything yesterday," they send a message that everything is a priority. People are left confused and uncertain as to which direction to take. As a result, there is a tendency to slow down as a means of coping with the stress and pressure that multiple priorities create.

Action. Do one of two things in every discussion: (1) Communicate your priorities and provide a "by when" date for delivery, or (2) give the other person accountability for these decisions.

Principle 4: Tell them what you want, not what you don't want.

Think Twice. Send a positive message that focuses on what you want, such as, "I need everyone to attend this program." Most leaders send a "what's missing, " "what's wrong, " or "what to avoid" message, such as, "I don't want to hear that people haven't attended this program." A "what's missing" statement leaves people feeling uninspired and focused on avoidance.

Action. Eliminate "what's missing" statements from your vocabulary for 24 hours. Replace them with phrases that tell people what you want instead of what you don't want.

5

15 Irritating Word Habits

How They Trigger Reaction and What to Do About It

Your Purpose

To communicate appropriately at all times by replacing **bad word habits** with **good word choices**.

One corporate communications exec to another: "The boss is tired of old clichés. We've got to get some new ones."

Executive Speechwriter Newsletter

Have you ever been distracted during a conversation by the use of irritating clichés or slang? Does it annoy you when people continuously talk about themselves? Now turn this around and ask these questions about yourself. How do you rate? Do you have word habits that annoy others? Most people do. This unconscious word usage creeps into our behaviors, irritates others, and affects the quality of communication. Because we are usually not aware of these word habits, we do not notice them, but others do.

Take the following quiz to discover your conversational tendencies. Then give it to someone who will tell you the truth and assess you. Read each statement and give it one of the following point values: 1 point—seldom, 2 points—occasionally, 3 points—often, 4 points—frequently.

1. I like to have the last word in a conversation.

2. I tend to generalize and use words such as *always, never, all, everyone.*

3. I like to talk about myself.

4. I avoid talking about myself.

5. Others tell me I don't give them a chance to talk.

6. I like to poke fun at myself.

7. When someone asks me a question, I respond with a question.

8. When referring to myself, I use the word *we*, such as "we're going to do that . . ."

9. Others tell me I repeat myself.

10. I have favorite phrases that I use repeatedly such as, "for what it's worth . . ."

Your Score: Add up your points.

A score of 25 or above indicates a high usage of irritating word habits. They are part of your everyday conversation. People can list and predict your offending word choices because they hear them frequently.

A score of 16 to 24 is an average use of word habits. They are part of but do not dominate your conversations. When you use them, people notice but they are less likely to react.

A score of 15 or lower shows an unusually small usage of non-colloquial and informal speech patterns. You have successfully managed to avoid the influence of television, radio, magazines, and other medias that use informal speech. Congratulations!

The Primrose Path of Misdirection

Most of us can effortlessly spew out words and clichés that we have picked up over the years. We simply repeat what we hear, and if we hear it frequently enough it sneaks into our permanent vocabulary. What's the problem, you might ask? No problem if the words evoke a positive response. But most word habits and clichés turn people off to such an extent that they stop listening. The meanings of words are obscure enough, without adding language that results in reactions and misunderstandings. By using jargon, clichés, exaggeration, and unnecessary words, we will be led down the primrose path of misdirection. Just because words pass into common usage does not mean they are commonly understood.

Word habits are unconscious behaviors. Some complicate the already complex problem of communication while others are just downright annoying. Language already has many idiosyncrasies without adding more. Word habits impede rather than enhance the quality of communication.

When people are irritated or annoyed by the word habits of another person, they check out of the conversation. And worse yet, the word habit can produce a strong enough reaction so that they will just stop listening. Poor word habits stand out and capture attention, but it's the wrong type of attention. Perhaps you attended a meeting where you heard a peer use a word that is commonly misused. She may have commented, "Irregardless of the situation." Bam: Just like that, you're obsessing on the word *irregardless.* Your mind is saying, "There's no such word—it's regardless." Your mind is editing and correcting her message while she continues to talk. You miss what is being said. Now think about yourself. Do you have any annoying word habits that cause others to miss what you say? It's highly probable since these habits are commonly often unconsciously used. You may have been annoying others for years. You would only know if someone had the courage to tell you.

The purpose of this chapter is to help you "clean up" your language by identifying annoying word habits and replacing them with good word choices. In the business world, many of these word habits go beyond annoying and can be quite deadly. Leaders must be even more attuned to the impact of language since their words are quoted, repeated, and published for mass distribution. As you read each word habit below, ask yourself, "Do I do this?" Then ask a coworker or friend who will tell you the truth.

Accountable communication is appropriate communication. Nothing turns people off quicker than language that irritates or violates values. Accountable messages are designed to inspire positive action in people, not annoy them. Inappropriate word habits get in the way of effective communication.

Word Habit 1: What About Me?

"What about me" people can be exasperating. You can't talk to them about anything but them. No matter how you engage in the conversation, whether you are upset or have something important to say, "what about me" people have a way of making the discussion about their life and their problems. The topic makes no difference. It's as if they have lived three lifetimes because for every experience you have, they have a similar one. You may be hoping for a listening ear on a sensitive emotional topic, but "what about me" people will soon be telling you about their woes. Or you may be talking about a difficult emotional situation you are trying to resolve and before you know it, they're telling you about the same problem but it is even worse for them. "What about me" people scream for attention.

When you are a leader, people reinforce a "what about me" approach by listening attentively to everything you say. This may lead you to believe they are genuinely interested: They think your jokes and stories are funny, your wit charming, and your life fascinating. Leaders can become seduced into believing that they have the ability to dazzle people with intellect and humor. To test this all we need to do is take away your title, position, and power and send you to speak to a group who know nothing about you. Watch their reaction. Are they as amused by your life and stories as your subordinates? Listening is a gift of respect that people give leaders. But they are listening because they have to because you have the power to influence their lives. The response you receive is less about your ability to entertain than it is a response to your power. A good practice is to observe how much you talk when you are with subordinates. Turn the tables and ask them about their life, family, and experiences.

Switching the Focus from You to Others

They say:	Avoid:	Replace with:
"I'm feeling down."	"It's funny you should say that—I am too!"	"What's going on for you?"
"I had a great day."	"Me too. I had a fabulous day."	"What happened that made it great?"
"I feel awful about . . ."	"I feel worse than that . . ."	"What exactly is bothering you?"
	Why it doesn't work: Each of the above responses has an exclusive "I" focus with no expressed concern for what the other person is experiencing.	*Why it works:* There is no "I" in any of these responses. A question is asked that focuses solely on what the other person just said.

Word Habit 2: Don't Get Too Close

Although asking about the other person and turning the focus away from you is important, it can be used the wrong way. A person who seldom talks about himself leaves others feeling uncomfortable. A "don't get too close" attitude generally comes from a person who does not like to self-disclose. Instead, the focus is on asking questions to prompt the other party to self-disclose. By interacting on a shallow level, we leave many areas of our personality, values, and beliefs inaccessible to others. Self-disclosure is what allows people to be authentic and real. When we self-disclose and reveal more about our inner world, people feel closer and more connected. Healthy self-disclosure is reciprocal. When it is one-sided, it results in an imbalance between people that often leaves negative feelings. When one individual self-discloses, she expects a reciprocal level of openness from the other person.

In one of my consulting assignments, there was a high-level leader who seldom disclosed anything about himself. People knew only that he was married, and they knew this because they heard it from others. They did not know if he had children, where he grew up, or if he had pets, hobbies, or activities outside of work he enjoyed. Although his credibility as a leader was high, his approachability was low. A leader's approachability factor has a great deal to do with inspiration and excitement. Approachability is what allows people to feel connected and close to their leaders. Appropriate self-disclosure is an indicator of a healthy personality. When a leader does not self-disclose, it creates a barrier.

⌗

Increasing Your Approachability

They say:	Avoid:	Replace with:
"I like to run three or four times a week to stay in	"Never got into it. Do you compete?"	"I'm not much of a runner but I like to cycle. I belong

shape. How about you?"

"My husband and I have two Dobermans we just love. Do you have any pets?"

"No, I don't but I've heard good things about Dobermans."

to a club, and we go on bike excursions a couple times a month."

"I used to have a Great Dane but she died a few years ago. I've been thinking about getting another dog: Should I consider a Doberman?"

Why it doesn't work: A brief, non-self-disclosing answer is given. No personal information is shared. The conversation is then rotated back to the other person. The imbalance in self-disclosure eventually creates discomfort.

Why it works: The question is answered with a reciprocal and appropriate level of self-disclosure. Both parties have an equal exchange of personal information, which establishes a comfort level.

Word Habit 3: The Last Word

Having the last word is similar to an addiction. People who have this need are compulsive about ending the conversation with their words. When they don't do this, they feel as if the conversation is incomplete and unfinished. "Last word" people miss or ignore the cues of others. The conversation may already have ended but they must say one more thing. It is not the content that is important to "last word" people; it's the fact that the conversation ends with them.

Leaders often have the last word because it is expected. You can change this. Ask others to summarize the conversation or close the meeting. Practice letting others have the last word. This raises the level of involvement and enthusiasm of others.

Ending the Conversation *without* Having the Last Word

Speaking Accountably

Example 1

DIRECT REPORT: "Thanks for your time. I know what I need to do now."

- **Avoid:** "Good. I want you to stay on track and get this done fast."

Why it doesn't work: You are either repeating information you already stated or saying something that should have been communicated earlier in the conversation.

- **Replace with:** "You're welcome. Call me if you need anything."

Why it works: It's short, to the point, and information is not repeated.

Example 2

PEER: "That sums it up—we've agreed to move ahead with the new expense procedures. I'll touch base with you next week."

- **Avoid:** "I think it's important to use these new procedures. They'll help us keep accurate records."

Why it doesn't work: Your peer ended the conversation. Instead of responding to this cue, you summarized (again) and had the last word.

- **Replace with:** "Sounds good. See you next week."

Why it works: You appropriately respond to the cues of your peer and end the conversation without presenting more information.

Example 3

YOUR BOSS: "This has been a good meeting. I like your thinking. I'll see you next week."

- **Avoid:** "I'll continue to work on a new way to implement our strategy. We need to move this quickly. See you next week."

Why it doesn't work: You kept talking instead of ending the conversation.

- **Replace with:** "Thank you. I'll see you next week."

Why it works: It's clean, short, and allows your boss to have the last word.

Word Habit 4: Tired and Worn-Out Phrases

Clichés are expressions or ideas that have become trite. Although clichés and platitudes become commonplace language, they are uttered as if they are fresh and original. It's hard to tell which is more annoying: the fact that they are trite or that the individual saying them acts as if he or she is imparting some great new wisdom.

⬦

AVOID Tired and Worn-Out Phrases	REPLACE WITH Everyday Language
• That being said . . .	• I think . . .
• To tell the truth . . .	• (No replacement—just tell the truth)
• At this point in time . . .	• Now
• At the end of the day . . .	• My conclusion is . . .
• When it's all said and done . . .	• My thoughts are . . .
• My two cents worth . . .	• A thought . . .
• For what it's worth . . .	• Ultimately . . .

- Having said that . . .
- Be that as it may . . .
- By the same token . . .

- Needless to say . . .
- All things being equal . . .
- That and a dollar will get you a cup of coffee.
- Just for the sake of argument . . .

Why it doesn't work: Predictable, boring, trite, and annoying.

- Despite . . .
- Similarly . . .
- (No replacement, just say what you have to say)

- Another perspective . . .
- Considering all things . . .
- (No replacement. Have a cup of coffee.)

- Let's examine all sides of this issue . . .

Why it works: Nonirritating, easy-to-understand words.

Word Habit 5: Talking without Periods

Stream-of-consciousness speaking, where one sentence flows uninterruptedly after another, is an example of talking without periods. It's difficult to imagine that the speaker even takes a breath while talking. It appears impossible to break in to the conversation. There are no natural entry points, no pauses or periods. In grammar, periods are used to identify the completion of a thought. For a person who talks without periods, their thoughts are never complete and therefore there are no natural pauses.

It's boring and sleep-inducing to listen to stream-of-consciousness speaking. It can put listeners into a trance, thinking their own thoughts. Talking without a point and avoiding the use of periods is one of the quickest ways to lose people's attention, along with your credibility.

If you recognize you have a tendency to talk too much or too long, you can employ self-interrupting techniques. More effective than having others intervene, interrupting yourself demonstrates an awareness and sensitivity on your part. It also allows you to take accountability for creating a pause so that others can enter the conversation.

Interrupting Yourself

Speaking Accountably

- "I need to stop talking. What are your thoughts?"

- "I've been talking too much. Any ideas?"

- "Obviously I'm excited about this, but I want to hear from you."

- "Enough from me. What about you?"

- "I've said enough on this. What's your thinking?"

- "I'm done talking. Your turn."

- "I'm repeating myself now. What do you think about . . . ?"

Why it works: You demonstrate courtesy, awareness, and accountability by interrupting yourself and inviting others to speak.

Word Habit 6: Whatever

Gibberish, incoherent speech, or a hybrid dialect is the definition of jargon. Like, Wow, man, that's totally awesome. Do you catch my drift? Slang and jargon can add fun and zest to your speaking under the right circumstances. They can also get in the way when people are trying to understand your message. In business, jargon can be used informally as a special communication between two or more people. But when it comes to meetings, presentations, memos, or other more formal events, jargon immediately reduces credibility.

Using Jargon and Slang
Speaking That Derails

- You go girl.
- What's up with that?
- What's happening man?
- Like wow, that's really cool.
- No way dude.

- He/she dissed me.
- For real.
- Whatever.
- Totally awesome.
- Am I right or am I right?

Why it doesn't work: Like, isn't it obvious? In a business setting, jargon instantaneously reduces credibility.

Word Habit 7: Filled Pauses

Unfilled pauses refer to the gaps between words or sentences that are filled with silence. Filled pauses refer to those same gaps loaded with fillers such as "uhmm" and "ahhh." These filled pauses are akin to humming, where a syllable or sound is stretched out to fill the space while the person thinks. They are meant to cue the other person that you're still talking or processing out loud. It keeps the conversation in your control. But it also makes you sound inarticulate and unclear. This is why an unfilled pause is more desirable than a filled pause. When you want to pause, use silence instead of filling the gap. Silence, used appropriately, significantly increases the perception of power.

Now, what if someone else starts talking while you are silently pausing? If you don't mind the conversation shifting to them, then it's no problem. If you want to keep control of the conversation, let them know early by saying, "Give me a moment to think about this," before the interruption. By doing this, you are articulating your needs rather than using "Ummmmm," or "Welllllllllll." Your credibility increases, and filled pauses decrease.

Increase Your Credibility by Eliminating Filled Pauses

- **Avoid:**

Ummmm	Ya know
Yea, ummmm	Ah . . .
Uh . . .	Oh . . .

Why it doesn't work: The speaker sounds inarticulate, unclear, and unsure.

- **Replace a pause with:**

Silence

"Give me a moment to think about this."

"That's interesting. I need to consider this."

"Good thought. I want to mull this over."

Why it works: Silence is much more powerful than a filled pause. Another option is to use a general statement that buys time, such as, "I need to consider this." It allows you time to think and yet maintain control of the conversation.

Word Habit 8: The Royal "We"

For people who use the "royal we" when referring to themselves, the word *I* seems to have become permanently lost from their vocabulary. You might hear "we're liking this" or "we could do that." They are not referring to themselves and another person; they are referring to "me, myself, and I." Used repeatedly, the "royal we" sounds strange to the ear and can be off-putting.

The word *we* when used to refer to oneself creates formality and separation in the conversation. Where "I" is up-close and personal, "we" is distant. It also causes the perception of authenticity to be reduced. The person sounds less genuine and intimate. Consider how self-disclosure sounds when listening to a person who uses "we" as a self-referent: "We like many outdoor activities." By using "we," there is no bond that self-disclosure normally creates, leaving in its stead a disjointed sense of the person speaking.

If you have the habit of using "we," just becoming conscious of it will help you replace it with "I." When you hear yourself saying, "We can see that," stop and correct yourself by saying, "I can see that." At first it may feel awkward, perhaps even vulnerable, because "we" has been providing you with protection and distance. If you want to help other people break the "royal we" habit, the next time they use it, ask with a sense of humor, "Just how many of you are there, anyway?" A few well-placed lighthearted questions such as this will raise their awareness in an amusing way.

Word Habit 9: Drama Words

Drama words are larger than life, overblown, and exaggerated. Superlatives and platitudes fit in this category. A well-placed superlative can bring home your point, but using too many will lessen the impact and is just annoying. For example, if you ask a person, "How's your day going?" you might be a bit dubious if you hear, "Incredible, unbelievable, it's an extraordinary day!" You are probably thinking she just returned from a positive-thinking seminar. Extremes in anything raise red flags. When superlatives and exaggerations are used in excess, listeners become suspicious and distrust the person talking. If everything and everyone is fabulous, others reason, then a compliment from this person means nothing.

◄□►

Superlatives Are Not Super All the Time

Speaking That Derails

- Very

- Incredible

- Fabulous

- Unbelievable

- Best ever

- Fantastic

- Awesome

- Terrific

Why it doesn't work: Everything is not great. Used to connote specific and strong meaning, superlatives are helpful. Used as everyday language, they lose meaning and turn people off. When something is good, say it is good, not great.

Word Habit 10: Self-Labeling

Self-labeling is the language of self-disparagement. Putting anyone down is not a good idea. Putting yourself down is not endearing or flattering either. Saying things such as, "Boy, am I stupid," may get a response of, "No you're not." But say it often enough and people will begin to wonder. If you need positive reinforcement, ask for it. Otherwise, self-labeling and self-deprecating remarks reduce the quality of communication.

Self-Labeling
Speaking That Derails

- "Boy, am I stupid."

- "I can't believe I'm such an idiot."

- "I blew it again."

- "What a loser I am."

Why it doesn't work: Diminishing your value and self-esteem does nothing for you, and less for others. Further, it reduces communication effectiveness.

Word Habit 11: Labeling Others

Putting other people down is degrading. It's similar to self-labeling, except the focus is on others. Language can add to this problem by collapsing a person and a trait together so they are one and the same. The word *is* and its equivalents are the culprits, for example, "He is . . . ," or "You are . . ." Using "is" or "are" collapses the person and the label into one identity.

Labeling Others
Speaking That Derails

- "You're an idiot."

- "You're crazy."

- "He's ridiculous."   • "He's stupid."

- "She's nuts."   • "She's foolish."

Why it doesn't work: It's demeaning, degrading, and devaluing. Plus the above words are "loaded" and produce a negative emotional reaction. Eliminate them all together.

Word Habit 12: Absolutes and Generalizations

Absolutes and generalizations stereotype a class of people, objects, or events and deny that there is complexity in the world. There may be a kernel of truth in some of them, but taken to an "absolute" extreme, they are no longer accurate and may be misleading. Replace absolutes, generalizations, and stereotypes with a word or phrase that qualifies what you are saying.

AVOID Absolute Responses	REPLACE WITH Qualified Responses
• All	• Many, some, a few
• All the time.	• A majority of the time.
• Everyone knows . . .	• Most people, many people, some people
• Everyone said . . .	• "X" said . . .

- Never
- Always

- Seldom, infrequently
- Often, frequently

Why it doesn't work: Seldom can we categorically say something is true or false. The above words represent an absolute condition, thereby greatly reducing the chance for accuracy, as well as eliminating any hope that critical thinking has occurred.

Why it works: Qualifiers allow room for exceptions and other possibilities. They represent a more accurate picture of reality and indicate that the speaker does not categorically generalize or jump to conclusions.

Word Habit 13: False Humility

"Aw shucks, weren't nothin'," said Jethro from the *Beverly Hillbillies* TV series. This might be acceptable speech for Jethro, but it does not bode well for leaders. False humility is interpreted as a manipulation technique to present a humble persona to cover up something else.

False Humility

Speaking That Derails

- "I've been blessed."
- "I've been fortunate."

- "I may not be very bright."
- "I'm not as smart as you."

- "It wasn't me, they did it." • "I'm a little slower than the rest of you."

Why it doesn't work: False humility is viewed as a technique or a manipulation. Even with real humility, a preponderance of these statements can be annoying.

Word Habit 14: Abrupt Interruptions

In a conversation, "breaking in" is legal. It's how you do it that matters. Abrupt interruptions by their nature discard or devalue the person who is speaking. You need a way to handle people who run on, talk too much, or do not get to the point, without embarrassing them. By making a statement that segues to what you want to talk about, you can rotate and move the discussion to another point or topic without diminishing the person. Replace abrupt interruptions with a smooth, more user-friendly approach.

✖

AVOID Abrupt Interruptions	REPLACE WITH Smooth Interruptions
• "Now wait a minute . . ."	• "That's interesting; now what about . . ."
• "Hold on a second . . ."	• "Let's pause for a second . . ."
• "I don't buy this."	• "Excuse me but . . ."
• "Stop. I can't listen to this anymore."	• "May I interrupt for a moment?"

- "Are you done?"

- "Are you just about finished?"

- "I need to take this call."

- "Just a minute."

- "I've heard enough."

- "Let me tell you something . . ."

- "I need to interrupt here."

- "That's an important point; now . . ."

- "That's too good to pass up—let's pause here."

- "I'm going to ask you to stop here and hold your comments."

- "Let's bookmark that and come back to it later."

- "I have enough information."

- Something I want to add . . ."

- May I interrupt?"

Why it doesn't work: These phrases diminish and devalue the speaker and derail the conversation.

Why it works: These phrases interrupt the flow of the discussion without diminishing the person. Smooth interruptions keep a conversation moving forward.

Word Habit 15: Finishing Sentences

This word habit involves either finishing a person's sentences simultaneously as they are speaking or bringing their speaking to a screeching halt. If you have this habit, impatience and/or an "I know it already" attitude usually prevail. When you listen to people, keep in mind that their need to be heard is paramount to your need to understand. Stated simply, let them say what they need to say. Speaking out loud is a way for people to process information and problem solve. When you interrupt their speaking prematurely, you may be short-circuiting their ability to think.

Key Communication Principles

Principle 1: Irritating word habits produce reaction, not action.

Think Twice. Word habits are usually unconscious and can be annoying. Just the repetitious nature of speaking in the same manner all the time can be distracting to listeners.

Action. Discover if you have annoying word habits by paying attention to how you speak. Develop an awareness of different word habits you have picked up over time. Ask others to give you feedback, and then listen.

Principle 2: When people are turned off by something you said, they stop listening.

Think Twice. When the mind is sidetracked by something, it focuses on the distraction. A word habit can cause people to turn off and stop listening to the content of your message. Instead, they are critiquing how you are saying something in their minds.

Action. When it is evident that your audience has stopped listening, pause the discussion and ask, "What's on your mind?" Although they may not tell you exactly what they are thinking, this will grab their attention and pull them back into the conversation.

6

When Your Words Get You in Trouble

How to Recover Quickly and Prevent a Repeat Performance

Your Purpose
To be accountable for your impact on others by **recognizing hot buttons** and **quickly repairing damage**.

There is no evidence the tongue is connected to the brain.

Anonymous

A wise, elderly woman is talking to a young man about his anger. "There is a fight going on inside of you," she explains. "It is a fight between two wolves. One is bad: full of anger, fury, and rage. The other wolf is good: filled with empathy, kindness, and compassion."

The young man thinks for a moment, then asks: "Which wolf wins?" The wise woman simply replies: "The one you feed."

Anger is volatile. Feed it, and it can grow out of control. How we listen to and perceive others is the fuel for anger and other strong negative emotional reactions. Our internal judgments about how others behave set the stage. For example, a person who whines and complains may be only mildly annoying to one manager while extremely aggravating to another. What accounts for this difference? We all have different hot buttons—emotional responses that are sparked by certain words and behaviors. These hot buttons come from our history, past experiences, and values. When they are intentionally or unintentionally pushed, the mind locks up and our word choices are reduced to emotionally loaded phrases and attack language.

We react when others push our hot buttons and when we push theirs. How many times have you unknowingly said something that generated a heated response? Until someone told you what happened, you had no idea that your innocent words could set off such an explosion. Intentional or not, anger stops all action and forces the emotionally charged feelings to the top of the list. How much work can you get from a person who is upset or from an entire organization that is reacting to something you have said? Not much. When people are upset, they are highly resistant, and they unconsciously slow down productivity.

The bad news in all of this is what happens to your time. Putting out fires and controlling damage takes up a lot of time. Once anger erupts, the only thing left to do is to recover quickly. You cannot ignore a negative emotional response or assume it will resolve itself. This only sends you back to the starting block where anger and resignation will resurface.

In this chapter you will learn what pushes your buttons and how you set them off in others. We will also cover what can be done to prevent negative reactions and how to recover quickly when prevention doesn't work. One good place to begin is by examining how the words and behaviors of others spark a reaction in you.

What Pushes Your Hot Buttons

Hot buttons, when pushed, can set off a range of emotions from disgust and anger, to a desire to physically take someone's head off. Depending on your background and personal history, some behaviors generate an intense response while others generate no response at all.

Acting or reacting with anger, frustration, or other strong negative emotions is automatic and immediate. Others say or do something that pushes one of your hot buttons and you react. It doesn't take much. It may be one word, a phrase, or a reaction to a comment that you made. Now you are angry and upset and no matter how well you try to hide it, it shows. Others react to your reaction. People are talking about what you said and how you said it. Before you know it, a chain reaction has occurred and the situation is out of control throughout the organization. Reaction to your reaction takes time and energy for everyone to recover. Preventing and containing your reaction are far more effective than cleaning up damage caused by words that have run amuck.

People are often not aware of what pushes their hot buttons because it is largely unconscious behavior. Something happens, and you find yourself reacting. Unconscious behavior is a default setting on our internal mental computer. An automatic response occurs without conscious thought or choice. Understanding what sparks these hot buttons puts you in control and gives you choice. Instead of reacting and producing a negative response, you can act and inspire others even in the most challenging circumstances.

Let's go to work to discover your hot buttons. Since the intensity of reactions varies from person to person, it is helpful to identify the four emotional intensity levels: No reaction, mild reaction, moderate reaction, and strong reaction. Read the following description for each level and answer these two questions:

1. What degree of emotional intensity do you experience internally?

2. What degree of emotional intensity do you exhibit to others?

No Hot Button—No Reaction: *You honestly do not have a negative reaction.* Those years of meditating on the mountaintop really worked. No response other than awareness of the behavior is evoked in you.

Hot Button 1—Mild Reaction: *You tolerate the person and/or the behavior.* You would rather not deal with the behavior but it does not provoke you to react. Every once in a while you might make a sarcastic comment in response.

Hot Button 2—Moderate Reaction: *You respond negatively to the person and/or behavior.* His or her behavior prompts an immediate reaction, and you respond verbally and non-verbally.

Hot Button 3—Strong Reaction: *You squash them like a bug.* Your "fight" instinct is activated, and you engage in full frontal assault. Your goal is to crush the enemy.

Now read the following two lists of behaviors and answer these questions: What level of reaction (for example, none, mild, moderate, or strong) do you have to the behaviors on List A? What level of reaction do you have to the behaviors on List B? Also, which individual behaviors, whether on List A or B, provoke the strongest reaction in you?

Which Behaviors Push Your Hot Buttons?

List A: People who . . .

- Coerce, pressure, and push

- Grandstand, show off, and try to impress

- Judge, criticize, and disapprove

- Attack and challenge

- Put others down and are derisive and sarcastic

- Dominate and control

List B: People who . . .

- Whine and complain

- Blame others and/or circumstances

- Talk behind others' backs, instead of talking to them

- Say they will "try" but seldom commit

- Publicly go along with you or others, but privately resist

- Do not verbally express what is bothering them, but make their discontent known through their behavior

Do you react more strongly to the items on List A or B? Or do you have a similar response level to both lists? The lists represent two classifications of behavior. List A is characteristic of bully behavior and List B is typical of victim behavior. Your personal values, history, and background affect your response to bullies and victims.

When Bully Behavior (List A) Pushes Your Hot Buttons

Bullies must reign supreme and hence engage in a top dog–underdog approach. In order to stay in a one-up position, the bully puts others down. The singular "I" or "me first" focus of the bully exemplifies the need to be the center of attention. Bully behavior is aggressive, dominating situations and controlling people. If the bully pushes your hot buttons, it may be because you have had personal experience. Perhaps you watched or experienced first-hand the damage that a bully can cause to self-esteem. Bully behavior may also conflict with your values of fairness and treating people with kindness and compassion.

When Victim Behavior (List B) Pushes Your Hot Buttons

Victim behavior has a "poor me, nothing is ever right" premise. Victims suck energy from projects and pull others down with their passive-aggressive behavior of dealing indirectly with people and issues. Their constant "it wasn't me" theme is represented by finger-pointing and blaming others. For victims, circumstances always seem to prevent them from getting what they want and need. Things happen to victims; they do not make things happen. If victim behavior trips your switch, it may be because it conflicts with your values of responsibility, emotional honesty, and integrity.

Understanding what behaviors push your buttons reveals valuable information about how you judge others. Wherever there is a reaction, there is a judgment. If a show-off who tries to impress people trips your hot button, it lets you know you also have a judgment. For example, "A person who needs to impress others is weak." It is the judgment that feeds the reaction. Every time you see someone who is a show-off, your mind automatically translates this to "weak person," and your hot button is activated.

Judgments About Character Traits

People who:	Are judged as:
Whine and complain	Weak, sissy
Bulldoze, pressure, coerce	Stupid, bully
Blame, finger-point	Victim, no integrity and/or accountability
Attack and challenge	Inadequate, no substance, all show
Do not verbally express	Dishonest, untrustworthy
Are sarcastic	Pathetic, useless, low self-esteem
Comply publicly, resist privately	Deceitful, devious

What are your judgments about people who exhibit List A or B behaviors? Your judgments feed how you listen and react. Let's say sarcasm pushes your buttons. You react to the behavior (for example, sarcasm) but underneath you are judging the person as pathetic and useless. Now we have something with which to work. How you judge others is at the source of your reactions because it directly impacts how you listen and filter what people say. Altering how you listen changes how you speak.

Prevention tactics keep hot buttons from going off—both yours and theirs. These are skills and techniques for listening and responding to people in "neutral," rather than being fired up. Most importantly, they sidestep the chain response of "you react, they react, you react" and so on. Stop reactions before they start, and you will have an environment much more conducive for effective communication.

Prevention Tactic 1: Listen with Positive Expectations, Not Judgment

To take charge of your hot buttons you must master listening with positive expectations. To be technically correct, people do not push your buttons; you allow them to be pushed by how you listen. You control what you hear and how you choose to respond. It is only a matter of focus, as the following story illustrates:

> Two men were walking down a crowded sidewalk. Suddenly, one man exclaimed, "Listen to the sound of the birds." But the other could not hear. He asked his companion how he could hear the birds amongst all the people and traffic. The first man did not explain. He simply took a coin out of his pocket and dropped it to the sidewalk,

whereupon a half-dozen people began to look about them. "We hear," he said, "what we listen for."

There are two choices when it comes to listening—we can listen with positive expectations or we can listen with judgment. How we listen shapes how we speak. Listening with judgment is an unconscious behavior. Once a judgment is in place, we listen for what we want to hear. If we have judged a person as stupid, we listen for everything that supports this perception. Unfortunately, education trains us in how to critically listen, analyze, critique, and evaluate. If your background is in law, finance, or engineering, for example, you have been trained in critical thinking. This is similar to judgment, where your focus is on what's missing and what's wrong.

Listening with Judgment

Outcome: To seek and destroy

Focus: What's wrong, what's unfair, what's inconsistent, what's insincere, what's stupid, what's missing, and what's not going to work.

You think: "Boy, is this guy dumb!"

You say: "That's the stupidest thing I've ever heard!"

Why it doesn't work: Listening with judgment is unconscious and automatic. While you listen, your judgments are at work filtering what others are saying. This makes you easily susceptible to having your hot buttons pushed.

Listening with positive expectations is a conscious choice. Instead of focusing on the limiting behavior of a person, you shift your focus to the underlying commitment and positive intentions. In other words, you separate the behavior from the person and concentrate on who the person wants to be, not how he or she is acting. Behavior is not the person. Behavior is only an expression of a person.

Listening with Positive Expectations

Outcome: To support and inspire

Focus: The unexpressed commitment, positive intention, and contribution the person wants to make.

You think: "She's very committed to making this work."

You say: "I appreciate your commitment and energy on . . ."

Why it works: Listening with positive expectations is conscious and deliberate. You choose to be positive. It is important to trust that others have positive intentions, even when their behaviors are inconsistent with this. Listening for the unexpressed commitment and positive intention of a person allows you to bypass your hot buttons and focus on the positive contribution that the person wants to make.

You are in control of your own hot buttons. First, acknowledge you have judgments of people. Second, acknowledge that you have stronger judgments about certain types of people and behavior than you have about others. Third, especially when you are with others whose behaviors set you off, listen for the unexpressed positive intention.

> **Before you react, stop and think:**
> *Underneath poor behavior is a frustrated*
> *commitment trying to get out.*

Prevention Tactic 2: Ask for Information in a Nonthreatening Manner

Another valuable prevention tactic is to understand what words provoke a strong distrustful, negative response. Sometimes called "trigger words," they evoke an immediate reaction by attacking and labeling people. These words also challenge competency, values, and integrity. They can be used in a close relationship where "Boy, is that dumb," has a mutually understood, humorous meaning. Otherwise, trigger words can be extremely touchy and are better avoided.

Words That Get You in Trouble

Speaking That Derails

Words That Attack Thinking and Intelligence:

Stupid	Brainless	Idiotic	Crazy
Brain-dead	Ridiculous	Pitiful	Athletic
Asinine	Pathetic	Mindless	Absurd
Senseless	Ludicrous	Preposterous	Foolish

Why it doesn't work: Strong words are typically used when an individual is upset and angry at a person's "lack of thinking." Delivered with a "you are" or "this is" preface, they attack, ridicule, and put down both the behavior and the person. These words also evoke a highly charged, negative emotional response and once spoken are imprinted in the mind of the other person.

Words That Attack Values and Relationships:

Irresponsible	Thoughtless	Self-centered	Crude
Inconsiderate	Unfeeling	Rude	Infantile
Selfish	Egotistical	Immature	Juvenile
Tactless	Heartless	Bad-mannered	Unkind

Why it doesn't work: The values of caring, kindness, and compassion are widely held. Words that attack them or how a person behaves in a relationship produce a strong negative response. When spoken out loud, the above words stick in a person's mind making recovery difficult.

The above words are a form of nonaccountable language. They are used to attack others and place blame on others instead of on ourselves, creating an environment of victimization and defensiveness. Besides, they are personalized and attack the values and character of a person.

Hitting Below the Belt

Speaking That Derails

- "You're crazy."

- "You're off your rocker."

- "You're talking nonsense."

- "You're being ridiculous."

- "You're nuts."

Why it doesn't work: When expressed as an attack, trigger words strike with the word "you" in the first part of the sentence. This targeted, nonaccountable way of speaking points the finger and accuses. People who are spoken to in this way will have to fight back or leave.

When the focus is on understanding, words that attack naturally disappear from our vocabulary. The spotlight is now on understanding, which causes the mind to access a more rational rather than emotive process. We watch for the intention, commitment, and key points. By concentrating on understanding, we use questions and comments that support the expression of an individual.

When the focus is on what's missing or what's wrong, the mind is intent on criticizing and evaluating. In this context, words that attack are activated and flow naturally out of our mouths because they are evaluative and critical. To minimize and prevent trigger words

from unconsciously slipping from your lips, alter how you pay attention. Make a conscious effort to focus on understanding what is being
said. Let clarity and comprehension be your goals before you respond.
This will help keep you out of trouble.

Remember, trigger words are automatic. Often, listening for
what's wrong activates them. When you change your focus, you
change the words your mind accesses. Below are questions and statements that keep the discussion aimed at understanding and gather-
ing high-quality information. These questions ask for information
with a nonthreatening approach.

⊐✪⊏

Asking for Information in a Nonthreatening Manner

Speaking Accountably

- "Help me understand how you got from 'A' to 'Z.'"

- "Tell me about your thinking process. How did you arrive at
  this conclusion?"

- "What am I missing? Connect the dots for me."

- "This is different from what I expected. Help me get a handle
  on the choices you've made."

- "Are we solving the same problem? I thought we were talking
  about . . . Where is your focus?"

- "I'm concerned about what you've said. We may be on different pages. Let me check your understanding on . . ."

- "What has prompted you to . . . ?"

- "What happened that caused you to . . . ?"

- "I feel like I've come in during the middle of the movie. Please tell me what's been happening with you."

Why it works: Questions and statements that focus on understanding rather than criticizing and attacking open up the conversation. By focusing on understanding, you gain information and insight on "what happened." This provides you the opportunity to work together and correct the current situation as well as a way to put preventive measures in place for the future.

The focus on understanding consistently stimulates accountable language. Again, if you change your focus, your mind will sort and select a different language. All language is logged in your mind, both accountable and nonaccountable words. The challenge is selecting the appropriate language, not remembering it. When you replace trigger words with accountable language, you are being authentic about how you feel without attacking the person. People need to know when you are disappointed or upset. You can express this by taking accountability for how you feel.

Expressing How You Feel
Speaking Accountably

- "I'm disappointed with . . ."

- "I feel concerned about . . ."

- "I'm bothered by . . ."

- "I'm feeling resigned and hopeless . . ."

- "I'm worried that . . ."

- "I'm anxious that . . ."

- "I feel let down."

- "I'm frustrated."

- "I'm upset that . . ."

- "I'm afraid that . . ."

Why it works: The word *I* signifies ownership and accountability. There is no attack or external target. The individual expresses what he or she is feeling, using the words of soft emotions (for example, *hurt*, *sad*, *disappointed*).

Prevention Tactic 3: When in Doubt, Leave It Out

If there is a nagging voice in your head asking, "Should I say this?" then don't say it. When in doubt, leave it out. This simple, straightforward rule will save you many headaches. People have different sensitivities in an ever-changing world. The appropriateness of our communication must change also. Swearing, off-color jokes, statements of prejudice, and sexual comments are examples of objectionable language. Do not take chances. Remember, recovery takes much longer than prevention.

Objectionable Communication
Speaking That Derails

- **Locker Room Language:** Swearing, off-color jokes, and other inappropriate language.

- **Prejudicial Language:** Jokes, comments, or references that stereotype race, ethnic background, gender, and so forth.

- **Deficiency Language:** You're no good, you're inadequate, you're incompetent, and you're useless.

- **Sexual Language:** Jokes, comments, and/or observations that have a sexual undertone.

Why it doesn't work: Objectionable language produces negative responses. Often used in humor, most people do not find anything funny about language that demeans others.

Prevention Tactic 4: Cool Off before You Open Your Mouth

It is good practice to cool off and disengage from anything provoking a negative reaction, before you speak. Sometimes you can delay your response for 24 hours or more. At others times, your delay may be seconds or minutes. As you will recall from earlier chapters, when you react in an emotional way, the mind shuts down. In other words, it is short-circuited and you are only working with a limited portion of your thinking ability. A delayed response gives your mind time to unlock and gives you access to more of your brain. You are then better able to communicate and generate options.

Cooling Off Guidelines

- **Take 24 hours and disengage from the situation.** It's amazing what time will do. Stepping back from the person and situation allows your mind to focus on a broader viewpoint. Anytime you expand your perspective, you discover more options. Your feelings about what happened or what was said may or may not change. What will change is your ability to gather resources and express yourself more effectively.

- **When you don't have 24 hours, count to 5 before responding.** Exhale and let go. Then if you need a few seconds to gather yourself, ask a question of clarification such as, "Would you explain what you meant when you said . . . ?" The question buys you time and the answer might be different from what you expect.

- **Notice your first reaction, but choose your second.** First reactions generally reveal our automatic judgments and most critical assessment of the person. They represent thoughts that are going through your mind. Just because the thought is inside your head does not mean you should express it. Give yourself time to uncover your second reaction. You may still be upset, but you will have better control over how you communicate.

Why it works: Cooling off puts you in control. It gives you the opportunity to "think and act" rather than "react and regret." It stops the process of you reacting, others reacting, you reacting, and so on. By cooling off, you alter your internal state and generate options for handling the situation.

Prevention Tactic 5: Talk "Now," Not "Always"

Put a frame around it: It is not "always"; it is "sometimes" or perhaps "often." Using universal words drives the mind crazy. When people hear an absolute statement such as "You always . . . ," they immediately begin to search for the exception. Rather than listening, they are trying to prove you wrong. It is unlikely that someone *always* does anything. When you frame the message, you are defining a specific time period when the behavior occurred, or taking accountability for how you feel right now. Qualifying phrases keep others from getting stuck searching for the exception or defending. They also leave room for a discussion about improvement and change.

Provide a "Now" Time Frame
Speaking Accountably

- "At this moment . . ."

- "Right now . . ."

- "For now . . ."

- "To me at this time . . ."

- "It appears this way to me . . ."

- "Today it seems . . ."

- "For the past couple weeks it appeared . . ."

Why it works: Qualifying phrases, such as the ones above, limit your comments to a specific time period. In the absence of a qualifying phrase, people interpret your message to mean "always" or "all the time," even without these words. Eliminate implied meaning and be explicit about what you are communicating. Define and limit the time period to "now" statements. People are more responsive and open to a "now" statement than an "always" comment. When people hear "always," they feel the task is impossible.

Prevention Tactic 6: Treat Undesired Behavior as an Exception, Not the Rule

When behavior is a temporary lapse from the norm, treat it as an exception. When an individual exhibits behavior that is unacceptable, you must first determine if it is a temporary lapse from otherwise good performance, or a serious downward trend. If the unacceptable behavior is a temporary lapse, treating the undesired behavior as an exception is appropriate. However, when this behavior is a serious repetitive pattern, a more rigorous approach is needed. At these times, it is necessary to hold people accountable for their results and impact on others. To learn more about holding others accountable, see Chapter 9: "Holding People Accountable." This prevention tactic deals with behavior that is a deviation from everyday behavior. Therefore, you can deal with it as an exception.

Consider the statement: "You're not being efficient at all in handling this." Even though the statement implies a reference to a specific situation, it is often heard as "You're inefficient." Without an explicit qualifying phrase, the implied message is often heard as "always" or "you are." An exception in behavior is easier to hear than a judgment about behavior.

Let's look at a specific situation. You are about to have a performance review with a direct report. Lately you have been unhappy with how she is running her business unit. The thought in your mind is "Your performance is completely unacceptable." This is an accurate statement about how you feel, but without any qualifying phrase your feedback will be heard as criticism and in a broader sense, an attack on her character. You can easily qualify your statement by starting with a positive comment about her usual day-to-day behavior. For example, "You are normally on top of everything. Lately you seem preoccupied." The first line identifies the person's normal behavior. The second line references the change in behavior.

> *Criticism is much easier to hear when stated*
> *as an exception, not as the rule.*

Feedback or criticism, stated in the context of a positive frame, is much easier to hear and understand. People feel validated and acknowledged. The new information is presented as an exception, a temporary lapse from normal behavior. Since your purpose is to inspire positive action in others, state your disappointment or concern as an exception. You then allow the individual to alter his or her behavior without embarrassment, shame, or feeling defensive.

State Your Criticism as an Exception

Speaking Accountably

- *"I'm your biggest fan. You always get things done quickly and efficiently.* Lately I've noticed your reports are arriving late. What's going on with you?"

- *"You are always direct and straightforward when we talk.* Today you seem quiet. You aren't expressing much. What's on your mind?"

- *"I like your enthusiasm and 'anything is possible' attitude.* Recently I've been missing this. I look to you for energy, but it's not there. Something must be on your mind."

- *"I've never met anyone as efficient as you.* During the past couple of weeks things seem to be slipping through the cracks. This is so atypical for you. What's happening? How can I help?"

Why it works: The first statement observes the typical, high-performance behavior of the individual. It is stated in the "present tense," never in the past tense. This is important. Listen to the difference: "I *am* a great fan of yours," or "*I've always been* a great fan of yours." The second statement carries an implied "but" and raises anxiety for what is to come. The first statement lets the listener know that this has not changed. The behavior change is then presented as an exception to the norm. To make this clear, a phrase is used to locate the event in time, such as, "recently, today, or lately."

Prevention Tactic 7: Take Emotions Out of Technology

Technology is wonderful—e-mail, voice mail, and the Internet have changed the way we work and communicate. Unfortunately, because technology has emerged so quickly, we have not had time to adjust and learn its limitations. Technology cannot do everything: It is not the answer to everything. And most of all, it is not effective for sending emotionally charged messages. Any message that has emotional undertones should be delivered face to face or in a "real-time" interactive medium. Do not use e-mail, voice mail, memos, or letters to deal with sensitive issues.

> ### Negative emotions and technology
> ### DO NOT MIX.
> *When you're upset, forget e-mail and voice mail.*
> *Use face-to-face or voice-to-voice communication.*

Remember the guideline "When in doubt, leave it out." If you are miffed about something and you think you are doing a good job of communicating effectively in an e-mail, think again. People can sniff out criticism, judgment, and reaction in any medium. Plus, nothing is ever resolved unless there is real communication, which means a real-time dialogue where all parties can express and respond. Used improperly, e-mail and voice mail are the reasons for many communication breakdowns and misunderstandings.

When the Damage Is Already Done

There are times when you just react and say something that produces an unintentional negative reaction in others. Unfortunately, you cannot erase what you've said and record over. Prevention is not foolproof. There are too many variables you cannot control, and sometimes things just happen. It is your choice to recover quickly and learn from mistakes to prevent repeat performances. At times such as these, you need the right words to take accountability for the situation and repair and rebuild the relationship.

This is what Sharon, a new CEO, needed after an informal meeting with a group of mid-level managers. Feeling the pressure to get things done quickly, Sharon remarked, "I want a 24/7 effort from each of you. Nothing less is acceptable." Focused on getting her message across, Sharon did not notice the exhaustion and strained looks on the faces of the already-stressed managers. Her phrase 24/7 (that is, 24 hours a day, 7 days a week) was an attempt to convey priorities and light a fire. She accomplished one of her goals—lighting a fire. Instead of inspiring positive action, her remark evoked strong feelings of anger and resentment among the managers.

What the managers heard was "I'm dissatisfied and disappointed in you. I want you to do what I do—work 24/7." They also heard, "Business takes priority over family and personal matters." Sharon's 24/7 remark traveled with remarkable speed through the organization. Soon other managers and employees were heatedly complaining about her unrealistic expectation. When you least expect it, something you say can spark an emotional reaction. It did with Sharon. As a new CEO, she now had an uphill battle to disarm the anger, demonstrate her caring for people, and reestablish her credibility.

> ### One Small Comment—One Big Reaction
> *A single emotion-laden word or phrase has the power to sweep through an organization.*

Emotional reactions are governed by a fundamental principle: Communication is the response you get. What you *intend* to communicate is not relevant—what is important is how others respond. You may think something you said was insignificant and minor only to find out later the entire fifth floor is upset with you. Others judge you by your behaviors, not your intentions. What you intend to do or say is all well and good. People pay attention to how they feel when you they leave you.

We have discussed two patterns of behavior: How your words set off others' hot buttons and how others' words push your hot buttons. In both cases, you end up with the same dilemma—an emotionally charged situation. When prevention is not an option, you need a way to recover fast.

The Only Recovery Strategy That Works: Taking Accountability for Your Impact

"I wish I had never said that" are words spoken in regret. Damaging words spoken out loud become anchors that drag everything and everyone down. There are two ways in which leaders attempt to recover from a "wish I had never said it" message. The first method involves the indirect approach: ignoring the reaction and hoping it goes away. It doesn't. Despite arguments to the contrary, time does not heal all wounds. Unexpressed negative emotions accumulate and eventually erupt. The direct approach—dealing with the impact of your message—succeeds every time when you are authentic and genuine.

> *Explaining your good intentions will not repair damage to a relationship. Taking accountability will.*

When prevention is not an option, recover fast. Use mistakes, especially yours, as a learning process. This reinforces an important message about focusing on recovery instead of perfection. No one is perfect, not even leaders. When leaders take accountability for their mistakes and undesired impact, it gives others the freedom to deal with their mistakes in a healthy way. Use humor when dealing with mistakes. For example, a leader made a mistake that became apparent to her staff group. Instead of pretending she did not make an error in judgment, she used humor. In a meeting with 200 people, she took accountability for her mistake and shared three things she learned:

1. It's just as easy to make a big mistake as it is to make a small one.

2. In order to profit from your mistakes, you have to get out and make some.

3. Why make the same mistakes over and over again when there are so many new ones you could make?

Her use of humor lightened the mood of the group and increased her credibility by making her seem more human and approachable.

There is also a specific cleanup process that allows you to take accountability for your impact. Read further and identify situations you need to clean up, then go and do it. There are probably a number of people who would appreciate a cleanup from you.

Cleanup Process
Speaking Accountably

- **Step 1: Apologize for what happened.**

  It takes just two little words, "I apologize," and yet these are sometimes the most difficult words to say. Other options include, "I'm sorry," "I regret my actions," or, "I regret my impact on you."

- **Step 2: Take accountability for your impact.**

  Explicitly state your accountability, such as, "I want you to know I accept full accountability the effect that my words had on you and others at the meeting."

- **Step 3: Make a promise about the future.**

  Make the correction to your behavior long-term with a promise about the future. For example, "In future meetings you can count on me to listen first instead of reacting."

- **Step 4: Recommit to the relationship.**

  State the obvious—that you care about the person and your partnership. For instance, "Our working relationship is important to me. I see it getting stronger and stronger, especially as we work through some of our communication challenges."

  Why it works: By taking accountability for your impact, you immediately put others at ease. This gives you a chance to apologize and tell them how you are going to put things back on track. By watching you take responsibility, it gives others the freedom to confront their own mistakes in a healthy manner.

Let's return to the example of Sharon and her "24/7" comment. How can she recover from the impact of her words? The standard approach would be for Sharon to explain what she meant. But explanations are useless when people are upset or angry. Before Sharon can explain her intentions, she must take accountability for her impact. By doing this, she diffuses the anger and clears the path for rebuilding relationships. Below are examples of phrases for recovering after the damage has already been done.

Taking Responsibility for Your Impact
Speaking Accountably

- You: "I owe you an apology. I have created unnecessary anxiety and concern in you. "

Why it works: You take accountability and apologize for your impact. The word *I* further expresses your ownership and accountability for the situation.

- MANAGER: "I was annoyed by what I heard, and I worried about whether I could work here given your 24/7 expectations."

  YOU: "I understand. I let you down and raised questions in your mind about having a balanced work and family life."

  Why it works: You are listening rather than explaining. The comment above reflects understanding and empathy.

- MANAGER: "Yes, you did. I want a balanced life, not the life of a workaholic."

  YOU: "That's exactly what you should have. I want you and every other manager to have a balanced life. When I used the phrase 24/7, my intention was to communicate urgency, not establish an expectation. I obviously failed in getting this across."

  Why it works: Up to this point, you concentrated on taking accountability for your impact. This is the first time you explained your intention. You are focused on understanding the feelings of the other person. The path is now clear and expressing what you intended to communicate is appropriate and useful.

Key Communication Principles

Principle 1: Communication is the response you get.

Think Twice. Your communication effectiveness is measured by how others respond to you. While your intention may be positive, if your words produce a negative reaction, you are accountable for the impact. Focus on how you want to impact others. Consider how your comments will affect them before you speak.

Action. Observe how you impact others. Keep an eye out for fires you unwittingly start or negative reactions you unintentionally spark. Watch how others behave around you and how they respond. If you notice a negative reaction ask, "Have I said something that is bothering you?"

Principle 2: Use the seven prevention tactics to keep hot buttons from going off.

Think Twice. Before emotions run hot, use the seven prevention strategies to diffuse the situation. They are:

1. Listen with positive expectations, not judgment.

2. Ask for information in a nonthreatening manner.

3. When in doubt, leave it out.

4. Cool off before you open your mouth.

5. Talk "now," not "always."

6. Treat the undesired behavior as an exception, not the rule.

7. Take emotions out of technology.

Action. Practice prevention daily. For one day try listening with positive expectations rather than with judgments. Concentrate on the unexpressed commitment instead of what's wrong.

Principle 3: Focus on recovery, not perfection.

Think Twice. Breakdowns and mistakes happen. When the damage is already done, you need to recover fast. By focusing on recovery, not perfection, you send a positive message about learning from mistakes. More importantly, you send a message that you are not perfect and you are willing to take accountability for your impact.

Action. The next time you make a mistake, drop the ball, or push a person's hot button, take accountability immediately. When appropriate, use the cleanup process and practice saying those two important words: "I apologize."

Your Words and How They Inspire or Derail

7

Talking Straight Responsibly

How to Be Direct and Handle People Who Are Not

Your Purpose

To steer the conversation where you want it to go by **insisting on direct** and **straightforward communication**.

When you get right down to it, one of the most important tasks of a leader is to eliminate his people's excuse for failure.

Robert Townsend

The lack of straight talk in organizations today is astounding. Employees do not speak up for fear of repercussions and consequences. Politically aware leaders are careful and cautious about what they say for the same reason—repercussions. Unless there is a crisis or something that catalyzes people and pushes emotions to the surface, straight talk is absent. As a result, productivity and efficiency are directly impacted. People dance around issues and do not ask for what they want and need. Grievances build, and in the end there is confrontation instead of collaboration.

However, talking straight responsibly is an essential skill in business today. Without it, employees are disgruntled and unhappy, and leaders are frustrated. The phrase, "If only you had told me" is commonly spoken *after* leaders are finally direct and straightforward. Talking straight is not easy, but it is necessary. If you want to get the job done, ask for what you want and get it, and eliminate the unnecessary drain on your time and energy. Straight talk is especially needed if you work with people who are indirect, noncommittal, evasive, or who withhold information or avoid closure.

Instead of being direct, many people stay stuck in the familiar rut of being nice and indirect until a crisis comes along that forces them to speak up. During a crisis, buried concerns, issues, feelings, and sentiments come spilling out. How many times have you watched this happen? A crisis becomes the motivator for action. This is what happened to the poor little frog.

There was a sad little frog who was mired in a deep, muddy wagon track. All his frog friends came by every day and tried everything they could to encourage him to get out. But the poor little frog was stuck deep in the mud, and he couldn't do anything to get out. Finally, after several days, the other frogs gave up hope and left.

The next day they found the little frog sitting by the pond bathing in the sun. He was chipper, joyful, and very pleased with himself. His friends asked, "How did you get here? We thought you couldn't get out of that rut." The little frog replied, "I couldn't, but when a wagon came toward me, I had to!"

The story about the little frog could be applied to anyone who works in an organization. It often takes something or someone to wake people up out of comfortable patterns and cause action. Why wait until a crisis? You can demand and achieve outstanding results by talking straight on a daily basis. When a leader is direct and holds people accountable for high expectations, people pay attention. No longer can they hide behind "no one told me."

Responsible straight talk inspires people. They experience a sense of freedom when they know there is honest and direct communication. It is important to be able to talk about expectations, disappointments, and execution. Without straight talk, behaviors do not change. Only when a leader is honest and communicates responsibly is there an opportunity for people to work together to correct a situation or performance issue.

A leader must be direct and straightforward to get action and results. In this chapter you will learn how to be direct and steer the conversation where you want it to go.

Straight Talk Defined

Most people do one of two things: They either speak their mind or withhold their point of view. Talking straight does not fit in either category. It requires using accountable language that fosters safety and collaboration while demanding action.

Talking straight responsibly is the willingness to be emotionally honest and accountable at the same time. Most people only do the former. They express genuine feelings by dumping their opinions on others without being accountable for the effect they have on others. Then there are those who have difficultly being emotionally honest so they withhold thoughts and feelings while leaving others guessing.

> **Speaking your mind is NOT straight talk.**
> *Talking straight responsibly is the willingness to be*
> *emotionally honest **and** accountable at the same time.*

Communication dumping and withholding are not talking straight. Both paths lead to communication problems too numerous to count with distrust, doubt, and suspicion topping the list. Leaders pay a high price by not talking straight, including low morale, mediocre results, and the loss of talented people. When leaders dance around issues, withhold information, or fail to provide clear expectations and closure, they lose points with employees. A determining factor in how others assess your trustworthiness and integrity is how straight and honest you are with them. People want straight talk and honesty from their leaders. Not surprisingly, most people handle the truth better than uncertainty, ambiguity, or dishonesty.

Straight-Talk Checklist

Emotional honesty is easier for some people than for others. It requires being in touch with what you want before attempting to communicate. The straight-talk checklist assists you in being emotionally honest with yourself. Complete this checklist *before* having an important conversation with your boss, peers, or subordinates.

✦

Straight-Talk Checklist

1. What is the current situation?

2. What is the desired situation?

3. What, specifically, is the concern, problem, or issue?

4. Who is the appropriate person with whom to speak?

5. What relationship outcome do you want from the conversation?

6. What requests do you have? What actions do you want?

Using the questions from the straight-talk checklist makes it easier to prepare for tough conversations. It may help to look at each question a little closer.

What is the current situation? The first step is to identify what is happening that has you concerned. Be honest with yourself about how you feel—are you disappointed, upset, or concerned? Do you feel let down? You can't communicate accountably if you don't understand what is bothering you. Make sure you can articulate it to yourself before you try to communicate it to someone else.

What is the desired situation? If you could wave a magic wand and make the situation exactly the way you want it, what would you see happening? What would you hear others saying? How would people feel? Once you can answer these questions, you will have a clearer picture of what you want. The three sensory channels—seeing, hearing, and feeling—can help you examine the situation from all angles.

What, specifically, is the concern, problem, or issue? State your concern in one sentence, such as, "I am concerned about the drop in morale of your group during the past quarter." If you can't express your concerns in one sentence, you're not ready to have the conversation. It's important to fully solidify your concern and reduce it down to the core issue before you communicate.

Who is the appropriate person with whom to speak? Once you have identified the problem or issue, the next step is to determine the person you should speak to who will produce the most powerful results. Make sure you are talking to the right person. If it's a performance issue, that's easy—you'll be talking directly to the person. But if it is more complicated and involves multiple parties, determine whom you need to speak to first, second, and so on.

What relationship outcome do you want from the conversation? Before you speak, determine how you want the individual to feel at the end of the conversation. How will you reinforce a relationship message? For example, you could say, "Our relationship is important to me. I want the resolution of this issue to strengthen how we work together." Identifying and expressing an outcome for the relationship allows the partnership to grow.

What requests do you have? What actions do you want? Once you know the outcome you want, make a request in order to get it. A request moves the conversation into action. Make sure you know exactly what request you want to make and be prepared to specify action, times, and follow-up. For example: "Would you join me at 8 a.m. tomorrow to meet with the head of Corporate Development to follow up on our report?" A request can also establish specific performance expectations such as, "I want you to turn this situation around by the end of the quarter. Can I count on you to do this?"

Use the straight-talk checklist to prepare for difficult conversations. It will help you clear your mind and state specifically what you want. If you cannot answer all six questions clearly, you may want to talk with a colleague, friend, or professional who will keep your confidences. Talking out loud and having someone ask questions can clarify your thinking by bringing unconscious thoughts to the surface.

Asking for What You Want

Learning how to ask for what you want is a critical leadership skill. Requests move the action forward. Learning how to make a request and manage the response you get are key.

⊷

Asking for What You Want

Speaking Accountably

- "My request is . . . by [state time]."

- "What I want from you is . . . by [state time]."

- "What I am asking you to do is . . . by [state time]."

- "The action I want from you is . . . by [state time]."

- "The results I want from you are . . . by [state time]."

Why it works: Most requests are ambiguous such as "I'd like to have . . ." Make your requests direct and clear. Be precise, stating what you want and always include "by when" so you have closure. Fixing a deadline or due date makes the acceptance real. Without it, someone may accept your request but not act on it for an extended time.

A request for action is only useful if you manage the response and get a clear-cut answer. There are three acceptable responses to a request: (1) Yes, (2) No, or (3) a counteroffer. Make sure you know what the response is before you end the discussion. If the individual responds, "I need to think about this," then you have a "no" response. Ask the person what it will take for him or her to say "yes." Is there something more you need to provide? Establish a time to follow up and obtain closure. Don't let your request float out there in never-never land.

If you receive a "yes, but" response, this is also a "no." This is an extremely important point: *A qualified "yes" is always a "no."* A "yes" response means "I accept your request and I will go into action." Any conditions on this response place the answer in the "no" category. Your life will be considerably easier, with fewer disappointments, if you remember the distinction between a true "yes" and "no" response.

Managing the Response to Your Requests

Speaking Accountably

After your request, ask for closure in one of the following categories:

1. Yes. I accept your request.

   "Yes, I'm ready to commit and take action. Where do we begin?" Confirm who, when, what, and where. Tie down details to make action real.

2. No, I do not accept your request.

   This includes "yes, but"; "I need to think about this"; "Sounds good, give me a little time"; "Yes, but with one condition"; "Yes, perhaps down the road"; "I'd like to do this, let me see how things work out"; and "I'll let you know."

3. No, I do not accept your request and I have a counteroffer.

   "I like your idea. I propose a different approach . . ." "You have my buy-in on the concept. I suggest another implementation approach."

Why it works: People are indirect about accepting requests and committing to a specific action. By managing the response to your requests, you will obtain a clear "yes," "no," or "counteroffer." Tie down all "yes" responses with a "by when" date.

Being Direct

When you speak, people listen for what you expect and what you have decided. An easy trap to fall into is failing to communicate when a decision has *not* been made. Instead of being direct, leaders hedge when it comes to closure because they are not ready to commit. There are many times when committing to a specific action is inappropriate. However, for these times you need to give people closure about not having closure. This may sound strange, but certainty about uncertainty works. It provides definition, boundaries, and a reality check on expectations. Being direct keeps people from feeling anxious.

Be Direct When You Have
Not Made a Decision

Speaking Accountably

- "*I'm not convinced one way or the other.* I am going to wait until the announcement on 'X' before making a decision."

- "*I'm undecided.* I need more input on 'X' before I'm willing to go to the next step."

- "*I do not have a decision today.* During the next couple of weeks, I want all of us to look at options before we make a decision."

- "*I am not announcing a decision or advocating a particular approach.* What I do have are recommendations for . . ."

- "*I have not concluded anything.* My plan is to gather more information and revisit this next week."

- "*No decision has been made.* And there are no plans to make the decision to move forward on 'X' this year."

- "*I am not ready to make a decision.* The topic is open for discussion and I want your input."

Why it works: Closure is crucial. The fact that you have *not* made a decision is important information. Leaders often think it is essential only to announce decisions that have been made. Wrong. It is critical to let people know when a decision (1) has *not* been made, (2) *will not* be made, or (3) *will be* made by (fill in the time frame). Minds function best with certainty.

You are the leader. You have authority. Unless you explicitly tell people you have *not* made a decision, they will assume you have and will decide what decision you have made. They will infer you have a fixed position and have made a decision even when you haven't. It is your job to clarify this up front, not at the end when their opinions have already formed.

Separating Facts from Conclusions

The ability to separate facts from interpretation or conclusions is a critical skill for leaders. Too often people confuse the facts and what actually happened is not clear to anyone. When you speak, divide the facts and conclusions into two separate pieces of information. Leaders who are descriptive and factual have higher credibility because listeners trust they are hearing an unbiased, factual point of view that is distinct and separate from conclusions.

❖

State the Facts before Conclusions

Speaking Accountably

Facts lead to	Conclusions
What I heard was . . .	What I concluded is . . .
What I saw was . . .	What I decided is . . .
What I observed was . . .	The action I want to take is . . .
What I noticed was . . .	What I propose we do is . . .
What I learned was . . .	I suggest that we . . .
What I discovered was . . .	This leads me to believe . . .
My research revealed that . . .	Based on this, I think we should . . .

Why it works: Disconnecting what you saw and heard from what you concluded keeps your communication straightforward and direct. Start with the facts and tell people what you heard, saw, noticed, and observed. Only after you have presented the facts should conclusions and/or recommendations be introduced. Use clear and direct language when you present your thoughts, such as "What I have concluded is . . ."

When you speak, decouple facts from your conclusions and interpretation of what happened. This will significantly enhance your credibility and believability.

Communicating in a Timely Manner

Ignoring something that concerns or bothers you is not a good idea. Often it raises your anxiety and builds distrust in the other person when you finally decide to communicate. Once you realize something is bothering you, sort it out so you can express your concern in an accountable and timely manner.

If you are someone who dislikes conflict and confronting others, you may allow an issue to build until it is emotionally impossible to ignore. By this point your concern has reached monumental proportions and may erupt into an overly intense communication or even a verbal assault. Waiting too long significantly reduces the option of using accountable communication. You may be so distraught that just saying what is on your mind is more important than how you say it. Your words may come out with too much force, leaving you in the position of needing to repair the relationship.

What if you have delayed communicating? First, examine why you have postponed talking with your boss or someone else about a sensitive issue. Second, communicate and take accountability for your delay and the impact this may have on the other person.

Owning Up to Delaying Communicating

Speaking Accountably

You: "I have been thinking about 'X' for a while but I have not talked with you. I want to apologize for not communicating sooner."

Boss: "Why did you wait so long? Why didn't you bring this up sooner?"

You: "I was concerned if I should say anything at all. I didn't want to upset you."

Boss: "Well, it upsets me that you waited to talk to me."

You: "Yes, I understand. It is my responsibility to keep you informed. We've always had a good relationship, and I want to keep it that way by communicating in a more timely manner. Are you open to having a conversation about 'X' now?"

Why it works: You immediately take accountability for not communicating. Additionally, you send a message about valuing the relationship when you promise to communicate in a more timely manner in the future. Accountability and correcting the behavior are two important aspects of this message.

When Others Don't Talk Straight

Identifying when others are not talking straight gives you access to speed and power. When you recognize something is absent, you can correct it immediately. Otherwise you have to rely on a more intuitive method for determining when an individual is being less than emotionally honest. You may get that funny internal sensation that tells you something is not quite right. If your radar is good, you'll pick this up right away. But remember, even though you know something is off, you may still not know what it is or how to correct it.

There are eight telltale signs that reveal when straight talk is missing. Do you know others who are guilty of these behaviors? How about you? Which behaviors do you engage in with (1) peers, (2) superiors, and/or (3) subordinates? If you're like most leaders, you will recognize that you engage in at least three of the behaviors listed.

The Eight Telltale Signs When Straight Talk Is Missing

1. Dancing around the issue

2. Dumping a laundry list of concerns

3. Dramatizing and exaggerating

4. Minimizing and reducing

5. Withholding information, thoughts, or feelings

6. Expecting others to read your mind

7. Dropping a bomb

8. Deflecting and avoiding

All of the above behaviors impede action and progress, yet they are common in organizations. As you read on, ask yourself: Do I engage in these behaviors and do I allow others to deliver indirect messages?

Dancing around the Issue

People who dance around the issue and hedge their bets never quite say anything that can tie them down. They always have an escape hatch so they can claim, "I never said that!" Used to qualify messages, hedging is sometimes appropriate and helpful. When used to avoid talking about sensitive issues, hedging can be destructive.

Hedging and Dancing around the Issue
Speaking That Derails

- "**Maybe** we can take a look at this **sometime** in the future."

- "**Perhaps** this is an issue we can discuss at **another time**."

- "It's **possible** we could move ahead **if** we see results."

- "I'm not sure **if** we should proceed. We **probably** will."

- "**For a while**, let's table this discussion."

- "**Conceivably** it's **possible**, if we think it through."

- "It sounds **reasonable**."

- "It's **plausible** we **may** act on this **some time in the future**."

Why it doesn't work: Dancing, hedging, and avoiding all have their roots in noncommittal language. Words such as *maybe*, *sometimes*, and *perhaps* are accceptable when used in contexts where they accurately represent a situation. However, when used to avoid being straight and honest, they get in the way. The previous statements illustrate two types of hedging: ambiguous time frames and a noncommittal point of view.

Hedging and dancing around the issue result in a lack of direction and closure. People need and want structure, direction, and certainty. When you hedge, you can expect performance to be less than optimal. Without clear expectations from you, people do what they think you want, not what you really want.

Following this train of thought, how do you handle people who hedge with you? At times like these you need direct questions that give you access to high-quality information and closure. If someone is unwilling to provide closure or make a decision, confirm this. This is itself a form of closure.

Handling People Who Hedge and Avoid

Speaking Accountably

- "When you say '*maybe*,' what exactly do you mean? What specific criteria need to be met for you to say 'yes'?"

- "When you refer to '*sometime*' in the future, are you saying by the end of this week, next month, or next quarter?"

- "When I hear you use the word *perhaps*, it lets me know you are not ready to decide. Is this what you are saying? When will you be ready to decide? What will it take for you to make a decision?"

- "When you use the word *possible*, does this mean (a) highly likely, (b) moderately likely, or (c) not at all likely?"

- "When you say my idea sounds '*reasonable*,' it implies you are not committed to acting on it. Is this accurate? What do I need to provide so you can make a firm commitment?"

Why it works: Providing choice is important when talking with people who hedge. The above questions are specific in nature and lead the person to respond within certain parameters. Just asking the question "What do you mean by 'X'" may not give you high-quality information. If the individual has been hedging, he or she will most likely hedge again when asked a general question. Going a step further and asking for criteria or providing a list of choices forces the person to respond with more precision.

Dumping a Laundry List of Concerns

It's not one thing; it's many. A laundry list of problems and issues obscures the real concerns. Too often, high levels of frustration cause people to spout off and dump one concern after another. When this happens, the person has not sufficiently sorted out what is really bothering him or her. Instead everything is listed.

❖

Dumping Concerns

Speaking That Derails

PERSON A: "I'm concerned about this initiative."

PERSON B: "What concerns you?"

PERSON A: "Oh, I don't know. A lot of things, I guess. For instance, you never copy me on any memos."

PERSON B: "Really? I didn't realize this."

PERSON A: "And it's not just that. I wasn't on the agenda for the last meeting, and you didn't discuss the topics with me in advance."

PERSON B: "Oh, I'm glad you're letting me know."

PERSON A: "Besides, you ignored the fact that I'm in charge of documenting the results."

Why it doesn't work: Dumping multiple concerns creates confusion and results in murky communication. If you start down the path of trying to handle each concern, another will appear. Person A does not know what is really bothering him or her. Therefore, Person B has become the sounding board rather than a problem-solver.

What can you do when people give you a laundry list of concerns? You can steer the conversation and hold them accountable for expressing what actually concerns them.

Handling People Who "Dump" Concerns

Speaking Accountably

DIRECT REPORT: "I'm concerned about this initiative."

YOU: "What concerns you?"

DIRECT REPORT: "Oh, I don't know. A lot of things, I guess. For instance, you never copy me on any memos."

YOU: "What else?"

DIRECT REPORT: "I wasn't on the agenda for the last meeting, and you didn't discuss the topics with me in advance."

YOU: "Anything else?"

Why it works: The direct report lists multiple concerns but not once have you dealt with any of them. Instead, you encourage the person to keep talking until the list is exhausted. This does two things: It allows the individual to fully communicate, and it diffuses the situation. Allowing people to say everything that is on their mind before you talk and try to solve the problem gives them the feeling of being fully heard and understood.

Once the concerns have been listed, you can steer the conversation where you want it to go by getting the person to discuss the undiscussables. Feeling let down and disappointed and talking about relationships are among the most difficult things for people to express. Instead, they take a detour and focus on tangible, easy to discuss issues. Take charge and gently intervene to encourage the person to be emotionally honest.

What to Say after All Concerns Are Voiced

Speaking Accountably

"I appreciate your candor. It sounds as if I have let you down. You're disappointed with my lack of partnership and support. Is this accurate?"

Other options:

It sounds as if I have . . .

- disappointed you.

- let you down.

- left you feeling unsupported.

- frustrated and upset you.

- discouraged you and affected your enthusiasm.

- unintentionally thwarted your efforts to move things forward.

- offended you.

- not listened fully to what you have to say.

Why it works: After the individual has expressed all concerns, you acknowledge him or her for communicating. Then you make an assertion about how you left him or her feeling. The person will either confirm or correct your assertion. Either way, you gather more information and move the conversation from an intellectual level to dealing with unmet expectations and disappointment.

Finally, a note of caution: Taking accountability for how you impact people does not mean taking blame. There is no discussion about whether they are right or wrong, or who is responsible. If people feel let down by you, they are. This does not mean you intentionally provoked this response. It does mean you are accountable for how you affected them. Focus on validating the feelings of others and find out what you did or said that contributed to their response. This puts you on the path of correcting, not protecting.

Dramatizing and Exaggerating

People who exaggerate make issues bigger than what they are. Dramatizing and exaggerating occur when people interpret rather than focus on the facts. They embellish their concerns by overstating what is happening. This complicates and distorts the message, making it difficult to ascertain what happened.

Dramatizing Concerns
Speaking That Derails

- "You won't believe what happened. I never saw anything so **ridiculous**."

- "It was **incredibly** bad, **very** bad! And **everyone** agrees."

- "I can't believe this **horrible** situation occurred! People are going **crazy**."

- "**It's unbelievable**, completely **incomprehensible**."

- "What happened is **mind-boggling! Everyone is up in arms** about this."

Why it doesn't work: Dramatizing or exaggerating involves evaluative and interpretative language. Rather than describing what happened and providing a factual description, the individual provides an interpretation. Loaded with expletives, every sentence seems to end with an exclamation mark. To the listener, exaggeration raises serious doubts about the accuracy of the information.

To handle people who dramatize, you must focus them on the facts and move them off interpretation. You can do this by asking questions that elicit specific, factual information.

Handling People Who Dramatize Concerns

Speaking Accountably

- "Let's start over. Tell me what you heard and saw first, and **then we can discuss what you concluded**."

- "Please describe **exactly** what happened. **Hold off on your thoughts** and let's focus on what took place."

- "I know you are upset and I want to hear how you feel. But first let's start from the beginning. Tell me **precisely** what was said."

- "What **specifically** did you hear?"

- "What transpired? Please be **explicit**."

- "What did you see? Describe the **specific** behaviors."

Why it works: Asking for facts rather than interpretation eliminates drama. Words such as *specific, precise,* and *explicit* help steer the conversation. Other key phrases, such as "hold off on your thoughts" refocus the discussion on facts. You may have to continually steer the conversation to keep the individual centered on describing, not interpreting.

Minimizing and Reducing

Minimizing or diminishing your own concerns is misleading. It also puts the other person in the uncomfortable position of trying to understand what you are really saying. The "Aw shucks, it weren't no big deal" communication deflects what is going on. The language of deflection reduces and redirects attention to other people and/or topics.

Minimizing Concerns

Speaking That Derails

- "Oh, it's not a big deal."

- "It's really a small thing."

- "It doesn't concern me much."

- "We don't need to spend much time on this."

- "It's just a minor issue."

- "It's really inconsequential."

Why it doesn't work: Understatement reduces and diminishes the significance of the message. There is also an unspoken expectation that others will recognize the importance of the issue and/or feeling without the individual being accountable for expressing it.

When you hear a statement such as "it's not a big deal," beware. This is representative of statements made when people are uncomfortable expressing how they really feel. How do you handle people who are indirect and minimize their concerns? Take control of the discussion and readdress the issue.

Handling People Who Minimize Their Concerns
Speaking Accountably

- "Let's pause for a moment and take a look at how this impacts you."

- "Before we treat this as a minor concern, let's reconsider what is at stake."

- "I'd like to spend more time discussing this. Even though it seems inconsequential to you, I'm concerned."

- "Although it may be a small issue to you, it's significant to me."

- "Before we act, let's consider how this will affect you down the road."

- "I want to return to your concern of 'X.' Let's take a closer look at this."

Why it works: Basically, you take accountability for bringing the concern to the surface and fully examining it. This reduces or avoids having subsequent conversations on the same topic. Just because a person says it's not important does not make it so. Make sure the concern is fully expressed and explored before moving on.

Withholding Information, Thoughts, or Feelings

No news is bad news when it comes to people who withhold. Being in control of themselves is key. By not divulging feelings, they are less vulnerable and exposed. In business, there are appropriate times to withhold thoughts and information, for instance, when you are dealing with a confidential issue or a pending business announcement. This is all part of being accountable and appropriate as a leader. It does not, however, eliminate or excuse the need for straight talk.

Dealing with people who withhold information, thoughts, or feelings requires that you take charge once again and steer the conversation. These intervention tactics allow you to control the flow and direction of the conversation by demanding high-quality information before moving forward.

Handling People Who Withhold Information or Feelings

Speaking Accountably

- "Before we go any further, it feels as if I'm missing something. **Is there something you're not saying?**"

- "It seems that something important is not being communicated. **What is on your mind?**"

- "I understand how you think about this situation. But I don't know how you feel. **What haven't you told me?**"

- "I've heard everything you've said, but it feels as if there is something you're not saying. **What haven't you communicated?**"

- "Let's stop the conversation here. Something concerns me. It feels as if you have more to say. **Talk to me.**"

- "I'm not willing to go any further in this conversation until I understand what is on your mind. **What's going on with you?**"

Why it works: Stopping the conversation and redirecting it to what is not being communicated challenges the person to disclose. Being direct is the best approach with a person who withholds. Eliminate the escape hatch of people pretending nothing is bothering them. Let them know you recognize something is being withheld.

Don't let people off the hook. They may answer your question with, "There's nothing more to say." That's a sure sign there is more. Probe again and be steadfast in waiting to hear the missing information. If the person does not disclose, say something such as, "I don't feel that we have closure. I would like you to think about this, and we can talk again on Tuesday." This alerts the individual that you are not satisfied or finished with the conversation.

Expecting Others to Read Your Mind

Some people believe giving hints, clues, and signs are enough for anyone to figure out what they are saying. The message is implied, but never explicitly stated. Expecting others to read your mind is followed by disappointment when they don't. The burden is on the person who must constantly work to get the other person to communicate. This places accountability on the listener to "guess" what is being said.

"Read My Mind" Messages
Speaking That Derails

- **Spoken Message:** "Everything is moving along well with the exception of a few snags. I'm trying to work through them as best I can."

Implied Message: Things are not smooth. There are problems.

• **Spoken Message:** "All things considered, I enjoy what I'm doing. All jobs have their ups and downs."

Implied Message: There are issues.

Why it doesn't work: The spoken message intellectualizes the issue and implies, but does not explicitly state, the concern. The listener is left with a lack of clarity and precision and must speculate about what is actually being communicated.

Dealing with people who want you to read their minds takes discipline and rigor on your part. You cannot let them slide by with unspoken expectations. Nail down what they are saying and what they expect of you.

⊏◊⊐

Handling People Who Want You to Mind Read

Speaking Accountably

• "I heard what you said, but I am not clear. What are you trying to say?"

• "It sounds as if you are implying 'X'? Is this accurate? I need to hear this in your words."

• "I'm confused. I hear you say 'X' and then I hear you imply 'Y.' Please clarify."

- "I'm hearing two things—what you said and what you're not saying. Let's talk about what you're not saying."

Why it works: When you intervene, you place the attention on the implied meaning. You are separating what the person said from what is being implied. By disconnecting these two messages, you can target the conversation to the part of the message that is indirect.

Don't allow people to put you in the dangerous position of reading their minds. This places accountability on you to provide clarity and accurate understanding of the message. Additionally, it gives the other person permission to continue being indirect and circuitous in his or her messages.

Dropping a Bomb

The thinking behind this is "If I ignore it long enough, it will go away." Delaying discussion about something usually does not resolve the issue. It only gives anxiety and uncertainty more time to build. An issue that surfaces weeks or months after the event is often seen as manipulative and dishonest. Although the concern is only temporarily withheld, the delay in discussing an issue creates feelings of distrust.

"Dropping a Bomb" Messages
Speaking That Derails

- "I've been meaning to talk to you about this . . ."

- "This has been bothering me for some time . . ."

- "I had hoped I wouldn't have to talk to you about this, but . . ."

- "This has been on my mind for a long time . . ."

Why it doesn't work: Each of the above phrases raises anxiety. If something has been bothering a person or has been on his or her mind for a long time, why hasn't it been communicated? The language is revealing and creates distrust.

When a person drops a bomb, it sets off alarms. The listener automatically gets the feeling that the "other shoe is about to drop." Trust drops with it. How can you trust someone who saves up his or her grievances and drops them like a bomb? Because they are unexpected, it creates even more apprehension. For the most part, people enjoy surprises, but not this kind.

Handling People Who Drop a Bomb
Speaking Accountably

- "Before we have the conversation about 'X,' let's talk about what caused you to wait until now to discuss this. Is it something I have said or done?"

- "I need to understand what has stopped you from talking about your concern before now. Did you think I would not listen?"

- "Help me understand. This has been on your mind for a long time. What have I said or done that prevented you from talking to me sooner?"

Why it works: Before discussing the issue or concern, the conversation focuses on the delay in communicating. The above phrases take accountability rather than pointing the finger at others for not communicating sooner. Asking, "Is there something I have said or done . . ." makes it safe for the other person to communicate why he or she has delayed in communicating.

The fear that employees have of speaking up is prevalent across organizations. A major delay in communicating may be the result of caution and distrust about the repercussions and consequences of speaking up. Your job is to understand what stopped the person from talking to you sooner and to make corrections so it does not happen again.

Deflecting and Avoiding

A common way to deflect and avoid an issue is to lead the conversation off track. Irrelevant comments or changing the topic completely is often effective if the leader does not reign in the conversation. In a meeting or one-on-one conversation, intervene and get it back on course when a person leads it off-track. Interrupting abruptly does not work. It diminishes the person, especially in front of others. How can you steer the conversation back on course? The following phrases provide accountable language for getting your message across.

Keeping the Conversation on Track

Speaking Accountably

- "Help me understand how your last comment relates to . . ."

- "We've been talking about 'X.' Please explain the relevance of what you are saying."

- "How does what you're saying deal with the issue on the table?"

- "I'm a little lost. Help me understand how what you are saying applies to . . ."

Why it works: The examples steer the conversation back on track and keep the individual from deflecting and avoiding. Without interrupting abruptly, you challenge the relevancy of the individual's comment and pull the discussion back on course.

Key Communication Principles

Principle 1: Talk straight responsibly by being emotionally honest and accountable for your impact.

Think Twice. Talking straight is not a technique to be used occasionally. It is a choice about how you want to do business. Being direct, honest, and straightforward increases trust, safety, and your credibility. Being emotionally honest and accountable at the same time requires you to be responsible for how your messages impact others without sacrificing being direct.

Action. How direct are you? Identify what stops you from being direct. Then practice talking straight responsibly on a daily basis.

Principle 2: Be relentless in demanding direct and straightforward communication from others.

Think Twice. It's up to you as the leader to create an environment where talking straight responsibly is expected. Modeling the behaviors you want from others is key. In addition, it is important for you to gently intervene and steer the conversation back on course when straight talk is missing. Challenging others when straight talk is missing helps people understand what they need to correct.

Action. Have a discussion about talking straight responsibly with your people. Educate them about the value of talking straight.

Principle 3: Intervene and steer the conversation where you want it to go.

Think Twice. Take charge and steer conversations where you want them to go. Without intervention and direction, conversations tend to go offtrack. The absence of straight talk contributes to this and keeps discussions from resolving issues and concerns.

Action. Steer conversations and challenge others when straight talk is missing. Do this in meetings and in one-on-one conversations.

Principle 4: A qualified "Yes" is always a "No."

Think Twice. Wishful thinking and a desire for an affirmative response lead many people to believe a qualified "yes" is a real "yes." It is not. Any condition on a "yes" response makes it a "yes, but" answer and immediately moves it into the "no" category. Just because you hear the word yes does not mean you received a positive response or that the person will take action. Accurately identify the response to your request so you can take the next step in getting what you want.

Action. Manage the response you get to a request. Make sure you have one of the following: (1) a clear-cut, unqualified "yes" with a "by when" time, (2) a "no," or (3) a "counteroffer" that provides other options.

8

Commitments
with Integrity

How to Replace Casual Promises
with Real Ownership

Your Purpose
To stretch and inspire people by **replacing "wait and see" attitudes with commitment**.

People are always blaming their circumstances for what they are. I don't believe in circumstances. The people who get on in this world are the people who get up and look for the circumstances they want, and, if they can't find them, make them.

George Bernard Shaw

Talk is cheap, as the old saying goes. But this was not the case in ancient Rome. When engineers were engaged to build what we know as the Roman arch, they had to commit to test it upon completion. The law read that the engineer who built the arch had to stand beneath it while the scaffolding was being removed. The point was that if the arch came crashing down, the engineer would be the first to know. Roman engineers understood that their commitment to quality work needed to be authentic since their lives were hanging in the balance. Given such high standards, it is not surprising to find that many of the Roman arches have survived for over 2000 years.

Committing with integrity—the promise to persevere despite tough challenges and difficult circumstances—produces outstanding results. How people relate to their commitments, whether casually or as a bond, impacts both people and results. Answer the following eight questions and take an honest look at how you think about, make, and keep commitments. The questions are also useful in a discussion on the importance of commitment with your group.

━✦━

Is Your Word Your Bond?

Rate yourself on a scale of 1 to 5 (1 = seldom if ever, 2 = once in a while, 3 = often, 4 = frequently, 5 = all the time).

1. Is your word your bond? When you make commitments, promises, or agreements, do you keep them?

2. Do you avoid making commitments?

3. Do commitments make you anxious or uncomfortable?

4. Do you communicate responsibly prior to changing a deadline or agreement?

5. Do you casually promise things you do not intend to deliver, such as "I'll call you tomorrow."?

6. Do you commit or agree to something out of impatience or frustration?

7. Do you promise or commit because it is expected?

8. Do others trust you to keep your agreements and promises?

Your answers to the eight questions reveal how committed you are to your commitments. There is no right or wrong score. What is important to discover is if you are steadfast in your commitments, both large and small. After all, it is easy to make promises but if you are not committed to fulfilling them, what's the point? Think about your answers and determine if you are one of the following:

1. **"No Promise" Person.** You do not easily make commitments or promises. In fact, you avoid them whenever possible. Commitments and promises make you uncomfortable.

2. **"Big Promise" Person.** Your success rate for keeping large commitments is high. When you make a big commitment, you intend to persevere and make it happen. You do not feel the same way about small or insignificant promises such as, "I'll call you soon."

3. **"Small Promise" Person.** The smaller commitments are easier for you. You feel more in control and less vulnerable and exposed when compared with big promises. When you say you are going to call, you do.

4. **"All Promise" Person.** Your word is your bond. It doesn't make any difference if the commitment is large or small. If you make it, you keep it or you don't make it at all. When you promise anything, your word means you will deliver.

All actions start with commitment, which is a declaration about the future you want. It is not about trying; it is about doing. Although a commitment does not guarantee results, it gives people access to their most powerful internal resources. When you genuinely commit to something, your mind, heart, and actions align to produce the outcome you want. Giving your word and committing to a specific action or result is what sets everything in motion.

Not only is your commitment important, but the words you use to make agreements and promises make a difference. Leading with purpose and direction requires authentic commitments from you and those with whom you work. Words are powerful; committed speaking inspires people to reach higher and do more than they think is possible. As Ralph Waldo Emerson said, "Do the thing and you will have the power." This is committing with integrity—using powerful words to declare the future you want.

This chapter covers how to use commitment-based words and phrases to inspire people to raise the bar on performance. Most leaders use incremental or "small-step" language that limits what is possible. Learning how to make bold commitments using quantum language will allow you to demand and get stellar performance. You will also learn how to eliminate wiggle room and obtain authentic commitment from others.

The Dangers of "Try"

Have you ever made a New Year's resolution that lasted less than 24 hours? Unfortunately, when language is used carelessly, resolutions and pledges are in reality "wish lists" instead of "commitments." We wish things were different; hope things will change, and try to improve. With all this trying and wishing, people feel powerless and unable to achieve long-lasting results. Circumstances—those daily, uncontrollable events of life—leave people feeling as if it's "me against the world." When people are in a "wait and see" mode, they use non-committal hedging words such as *sometimes*, *perhaps*, and *maybe*, along with other weak words such as *try*.

Language shapes our reality, and the words we choose have a direct impact on what happens or doesn't happen. Every time we "try" or "wish" things were different, we reduce our chances for getting what we want. Have you ever read the dictionary definition of the word *try*? It is "to attempt, to make an effort, to struggle, to do something without much expectation of success." "Try" is a trap: It is an incomplete action and a noncommitment word. When people say they are going to try to do something, it means they are going to make an attempt. The act of trying is a process, not an end result.

When the word *try* is used, it not only expresses a lack of commitment but it impacts how we think and behave. When you try to do something, it puts you in the state of "let's wait and see if this is a good idea." Being stuck in the "land of trying" steals energy and destroys spirit. Unless you only intend to make an attempt, the word *try* leads down a path fraught with obstacles.

If *try* is a word you frequently use, pay attention to how you feel about making binding agreements. Do you feel boxed in, stuck, or trapped? Many people think that commitments are limiting and take away choice. Interestingly, the exact opposite is true. The condition of trying is limiting and stagnant, while making a commitment opens up countless possibilities.

It is also interesting to note that the English language has numerous word combinations and jargon that have a similar meaning to the word *try*. In contrast, there are far fewer words that signify commitment.

Refuse to Be Seduced by "TRY"

Speaking That Derails

- "I'll try."
- "I'll try hard."
- "I'll try my best."
- "I'll do all I can."
- "I'll give it my all."
- "I'll make a supreme effort."
- "I'll pull out all the stops."
- "I'll bend over backwards."
- "I'll give it my best shot."
- "I'll make an effort to . . ."
- "I'll make every effort to . . ."
- "I'll take a crack at . . ."
- "I'll do my utmost."
- "I'll take a stab at it."
- "I'll go all-out."
- "I'll have a go at it."

- "I'll work hard."
- ""I'll endeavor to . . ."
- "I'll attempt to . . ."
- "I'll take a shot at it."

Why it doesn't work: Phrases such as "I'll pull out all the stops" sound good, but what do they mean? They come from the family of "try" and represent an attempt to act, but not a promise. The word *try* is not a commitment: It is appropriate only if you are communicating that you will attempt something. However, "try" is often used as a substitute for committing. "Try" and its friends are a form of indirect communication signifying minimal accountability for results. Using "try" hedges all bets from the start.

Another limiting aspect to the word *try* is how it affects the mind. "Try" is a mental condition that signals the brain to endeavor, not do, something. What happens when you "try" to lose weight, "try" to take a vacation, or "try" to work fewer hours? The likelihood of success is not very good. By eliminating the word *try* and replacing it with committed language, your success rate significantly increases. Instead of *trying*, you can say, "I will lose 10 pounds by . . . ," "I will take a vacation by . . . ," or "Starting this week, I will complete my work by . . ."

The mind responds differently to a committed action. A commitment means "playing to win." *Trying* means "playing to avoid losing." There is considerable distance between these two end states. The first requires full effort; the latter requires jockeying for position to be at least one step above those who lose. Of course, empty or meaningless commitments, regardless of the words used, do not produce results. The positive and real intent to deliver must be present. When your word is your bond, committed language is far more powerful than "try" and its friends.

Commit and Do It

Speaking Accountably

- "I promise . . ."
- "I commit . . ."
- "I will . . ."
- "I give you my word . . ."
- "You can count on me to . . ."
- "I will make it happen."
- "I will take care of . . ."
- "I will be accountable for . . ."

Why it works: The language of commitment is powerful and action-oriented. It unequivocally sends an "I will" versus "I'll try" message. These phrases tell the listener you are giving your word and that you can be counted on to keep it. A word of caution: Only use the above phrases for commitments you intend to keep. If you use committed language indiscriminately and fail to fulfill your promises, others will observe your behavior and discount your words. Overuse and misuse of the above phrases renders them meaningless and powerless.

The language of commitment is strong and direct with a message of, "I personally accept accountability for producing this result." Here is a case when using "I" is not only appropriate, it is necessary. Commitments require personal accountability even when involving a team or group. Speaking in the first person and accepting responsibility makes the commitment credible and believable.

Committing with Integrity

People commit too easily when they do not intend to deliver, and fail to commit when they intend to follow through. There is a great deal of laziness in how we use language to effortlessly make promises. We are undisciplined in how we speak about committed action. Promises, agreements, and commitments have lost meaning in a world where the word of a person is no longer enough. We question whether we can trust commitments. We doubt if we can count on people to do what they say. We speculate if their commitment is short term or long term. Will it last over time? We are skeptical whether the words of commitment will turn into action.

Are you undisciplined in saying what you mean and meaning what you say? Don't answer this question too quickly. There are many commitments and promises, small and large, which we utter without conscious awareness. We mechanically use numerous words and phrases that are socially acceptable but meaningless. Consider the automatic, innocuous comments that our language has become filled with such as, "Let's have lunch sometime," or, "I'll call you soon." Most everyone recognizes these as throwaway remarks frequently used when people do not know what to say or they want to exit a conversation. They are not authentic promises and commitments. Unfortunately, this is the problem. We are in the practice of using language casually and committing to things we never intend to do. Or, we have good intentions but do not follow through.

Casual Promises That Erode Your Word
Speaking That Derails

- "I'll call you soon."

- "We'll have to do this again."

- "Let's do this again sometime."

- "I'll e-mail you."

- "Let's have lunch before long."

- "I'll talk to you sometime soon."

- "Let's talk in the not-too-distant future."

- "Let's touch base soon."

Why it doesn't work: Throwaway promises are typically used at the end of a conversation. Meaningless and vague, they lack a specific time frame and intention to perform. Words such as *soon* or *sometime* imply meaning while promising nothing. Overused and automatic, these statements elicit distrust and are met with an unspoken response of, "Yeah, sure, I'll believe it when I see it."

At the end of a discussion, you may not want to commit to a future conversation or meeting. In this case, use phrases such as "I appreciate our time together" or "Thank you for your input." This way you can provide closure without introducing an empty promise you have no intention of fulfilling.

In the arena of commitments, there are no compromises. You either commit or not. As a leader, your words must consistently reflect what you truly mean. If you want language to work for you and inspire positive action, make commitments and promises carefully. People need to trust what you say and know your word is your bond. They listen to your promises, watch your actions, and then conclude if they can trust you. When your commitments are inconsistent with your behavior, people discount what you say. In the hallways, employees will comment, "Big deal—she said it would be done but her words don't mean anything." This is a reputation you do not want. When you lose the power of words, you lose the power to influence and engage people.

❖

Commit Only When You Intend to Deliver

Speaking Accountably

- "It's important for us to meet regularly. I will set up a weekly meeting."

- "I'll call you no later than Friday."

- "Let's have lunch to discuss the actions we need to take. I will call you this week to schedule a date."

- "I will follow up with you before our next quarterly meeting."

- "Let's talk every other week to update each other."

Why it works: In these examples, the phrase "I will" means "I promise." Also, a specific time frame is provided, which strengthens the commitment and makes it more believable. However, a promise is only real when it turns into action.

An organization is the expression of a leader's commitment. If the leader vacillates on making commitments or fails to deliver, people lose faith and the organization loses momentum. A commitment represents the gateway to a new future. Being disciplined about the agreements you make is far better than being known as a leader who does not keep his or her word.

Committing with Integrity
The Rules

1. Only make commitments and promises you plan to keep.

2. Replace "I'll try" with "I will" or do not commit.

3. Speak your commitments publicly. Take a stand.

4. Recommit when adversity strikes. Remain steadfast in your resolve.

5. Make it real. Specify when, where, who, what, and how.

In a leadership position, your word must be your bond. All you have is your word. Once people stop believing you, tremendous power and influence are lost. Back up your commitments with consistent, positive action.

Finally, a note of caution: There are times when the smart thing to do is break a commitment. Perhaps you have received more information or there has been a change in direction that necessitates reexamining a situation. At times such as these, it is appropriate and wise to responsibly break or alter an agreement. The best way to do this is in advance of the deadline. If you have a report that is due on Friday and you know you are not going to make it, advise all parties involved on Monday. Announcing a change in commitment or breaking a commitment after deliverables are due is not accountable. There may be extenuating circumstances, but this should be an exception. You must also be responsible for your impact on others. If you alter an agreement, check and see how this impacts other parties. Always check the relationship and make sure it is intact when you break a commitment.

Taking a Leap of Faith

Be bold when it comes to commitments. Reach for what may appear to be impossible. Will Rogers once said, "Why not go out on a limb, that's where all the fruit is." Commitments give you access to the fruit by driving actions. The larger the pledge, the greater the possibility for results. Bold commitments involve risk because your reputation is at stake. When you introduce a new change initiative, for instance, and make promises about intended results, your word is on the line. Nothing happens without taking a leap of faith. A commitment of any magnitude requires you to face the unknown. You must be willing to be comfortable even when you don't have all the answers. This is common in any major undertaking. Visionary leaders must be prepared to step into unfamiliar territory.

The beginning of anything always depends on the willingness of one person to believe in something others cannot see. For something to come into existence, it must be expressed in language. We create the future with words and build a picture with commitment. At times it requires that leaders be unreasonable and take a leap of faith.

Many reasonable managers and leaders are sensible, levelheaded, and boring. They do not inspire people. They focus on incremental steps of improvement. This works as a day-to-day tactic, but as an overall leadership strategy it misses the mark. People want to be inspired. Incremental steps and uninspiring language do not cause people to reach higher. Instead, it reinforces standing in the same place. At best the status quo is improved, but no change of any scale occurs.

The Language of Incremental Steps
Speaking That Derails

Small Steps:

- Improve
- Increase
- Recover
- Advance
- Better
- Enhance
- Develop
- Expand
- A cut above
- One step at a time

Weak Personal Commitment:

- I believe
- I think
- I suppose
- I assume

- It's possible
- I consider
- I guess
- I imagine

Why it doesn't work: Incremental language is useful for explaining and describing. It is not useful for inspiring and motivating. This type of language for improving and getting better provides people with direction but seldom lets loose the creative and boundless energy of people. If you use language that asks for incremental improvement, incremental improvement is what you will get. In addition, weak personal commitments support small steps. They send a message about "low-risk" and "caution."

Bold commitments require big leaps and the use of words that match. Taking a leap of faith and speaking in quantum rather than incremental language gives leaders a superior tool for mobilizing small and large groups of people.

The Big Leaps of Quantum Language

Speaking Accountably

Big Leaps:

- Dramatically change . . .
- Significantly alter . . .
- Create unprecedented . . .
- Surpass all others . . .

- Lead the market . . .

- No. 1 in . . .

- The courage to be different and . . .

- Reaching higher

- Raising the bar

- Upping the ante

- Going far beyond . . .

- Achieve greatness . . .

- Produce extraordinary results . . .

Powerful Personal Commitment:

- We will.

- This will happen.

- My resolve is steadfast and unwavering.

- We will win.

- We will succeed.

- There is no doubt in my mind.

Why it works: The conviction and resolve of a leader significantly impacts others. Especially when people are in a "wait and see" mode, leaders need to create a compelling future that engages everyone. It is the passion, determination, and confidence of the leader that lights the path for others. Language that represents a big leap causes people to take notice and stretch themselves personally.

Using bold commitments tackles issues that appear to be improbable or impossible. When you contrast the same commitment spoken in weak language, it is amazing to note the difference words make in generating a new reality. Leaders can speak the future into existence by appropriately making commitments with courage.

Bold Commitments That Inspire Others
Speaking Accountably

- **Weak:** "It is important for us to *improve* and *do better* as an organization. I would like to *explore* how we can accomplish this."

  Bold: "Nothing is accomplished alone. It is only in partnership that we accomplish extraordinary things. *Together we will create an organization that is unstoppable.*"

- **Weak:** "I am *hopeful* we can *increase* our performance levels by working together and *developing a plan* to improve our bottom line."

  Bold: "How we choose to play the game determines our chances for success. The question is—are we willing to dare greatly and create an environment that challenges each of us to perform at our highest levels? *I can't do it alone. But together we will make this happen.*"

- **Weak:** "I *think it's possible* for us to *increase* our visibility in our industry. My thoughts are to reexamine how we do business."

  Bold: "We have only one priority in front of us—to increase our visibility. Together we will change the direction and shape of our company. *We will be the best in our industry and the envy of others.*"

- **Weak:** "I'm not sure how to proceed. Let's brainstorm and see what we *may* be able to accomplish."

  Bold: "I don't have all the answers. I cannot tell you exactly how we will surpass our objectives. I do not know what we will encounter. *But I do know this—we will succeed and be No. 1 in . . .*"

Why it works: The leader takes an unmistakable stand and makes a clear commitment to the future. There is no hedging, wiggle room, or implied retreat. The strong "We will make it happen" message mobilizes and inspires people to reach higher and raise the bar on performance.

Committing to the Personal Success of Others

One of the most powerful leadership skills you can acquire is expressing your commitment to the success of others. Committing to the success of an individual is a personal promise that focuses on career path and aspirations. People need to know you are personally committed to them. Saying it once, or implying it, is not sufficient. Especially during times of major change and uncertainty, people need to know you support them and have their best interests at heart. Look for opportunities to express your commitment to their success both privately and in groups.

When you commit to the success of others, you are letting them know you will support them *in all ways*. Your language is critical and needs to paint a visual picture of all of you standing side by side facing challenges together.

"We're in This Together" Language

Speaking Accountably

- "You can count on me . . ."

- "I am committed to your success . . ."

- "I want you to know that I will work with you to . . ."

- "I will stand beside you . . ."

- "Together we will . . ."

- "I will partner with you to make this happen."

- "No matter what happens, you can count on my support."

- "You are not alone. I consider this to be 'our' challenge."

- "I'm your partner in this. Together we will . . ."

- "I support you 100 percent and I will let others know where I stand."

Why it works: If you want people to take risks, stretch, and make bold commitments, they need to know you are standing beside them. People are inspired by phrases that communicate they are not alone in facing the unknown. They need to know you are their partner.

Verbally expressing your commitment to the success of others inspires positive action. When people know, without a doubt, that they have your support and partnership, unprecedented results can be produced. But you must say it out loud. Thinking and implying that you are committed to the success of others is not good enough. Tell people you are committed to their success and be specific so they know what you envision for their future.

Committing to the Success of Others

Speaking Accountably

SUBORDINATE: "I would like to head up the new initiative but I don't know if I'm ready for this. I don't have any experience leading groups."

YOU: "I hear your concerns. I want you to know I don't have any concerns about your ability. I know you can do it well."

SUBORDINATE: "But I'm not sure I can get everyone's support. There is a lot of resistance to my taking charge especially since others senior to me want this position."

You: "That's true. Here's what you can count on me to do. I will work with you to break down the resistance and effectively position you with the other business units."

Subordinate: "And what if I encounter major challenges?"

You: "I will stand right beside you. Together we'll make this work. I am committed to your development and I will provide you with whatever opportunities are important for your growth."

Why it works: The above dialogue reaffirms your belief in the individual by explicitly committing to his or her growth and development. Verbally articulating your commitment to the success of others inspires positive action. People need reaffirmation that you are committed to their personal success regardless of your aspirations.

Look for opportunities to express your commitment to the success of others. You cannot say it enough. Don't wait for an organizational change or responsibilities to shift before you let people know you are committed to their success. People need to know you are behind them every step of the way. Let them know you are personally committed to them and demonstrate it in your behaviors.

Inspiring Commitment in Others

Most people prefer a supportive boss who is demanding instead of one who accommodates and excuses less-than-stellar performance. People want to grow, stretch, and contribute to something meaningful and compelling. Being unreasonable in demanding the best from people raises the bar. When you are too reasonable you excuse, explain, and rationalize mediocre performance. Or you may settle for good performance when it could be great performance. Being demanding is part of being a leader. Your job is to up the ante and stretch and inspire people to reach higher.

Commitments are a powerful tool. They can move people to new levels of performance beyond what they thought possible. A sense of ownership, along with definite time frames, spurs high levels of performance. Many people avoid making commitments or they make vague promises. Your job is to make sure people declare and perform against powerful, explicit, and authentic commitments. Commitments establish precise expectations. Some people will be uncomfortable when you press them on their commitments. Tension rises when specific expectations are nailed down. When terms and conditions are clear, it is much easier to hold people accountable and spot breakdowns and problems.

Use the following guidelines to ensure that an authentic and complete commitment is being made. You can use these questions for both yourself and others. The guidelines serve as a reality check to make sure all elements of the commitment are present.

Perform a Reality Check on Commitments

Determine If the Commitment Is Authentic:

1. Is this a promise or agreement you are willing to keep?

2. Is this commitment consistent with your priorities (at work and home) and with your values?

3. Are you willing to publicly declare your commitment (for example, in a meeting, with coworkers, and so forth)?

Determine If All Elements Are Present:

1. What are the specific parameters of your commitment? When will it be completed? How will you accomplish this? Who will be involved? What is needed? Where will this take place?

2. How will you measure your success?

3. Who are your partners in supporting you on this commitment?

If you accept an incomplete commitment, you are accountable for the lack of results. It is your job to make sure commitments are complete, well-structured, and translated into deliverables by tying down timing and implementation. Expecting a partial or incomplete commitment to be fulfilled will lead to disappointment.

> *By managing commitments, you manage results.*

By managing commitments, you manage results and bring out the best in people. Managers and leaders who are committed to bringing out the best in people and giving the best of themselves inspire high levels of performance. Although commitment does not guarantee results, results do not happen without it. Most people have a need to do their best; the rest depends on environment and their relationship with those who directly impact their career, especially their boss. People give what they are inspired to give. This is your job as a leader—to inspire positive action in people.

Eliminating Wiggle Room

All too often, people build wiggle room into commitments and agreements. This is defined as "an incomplete communication in which there is room for multiple interpretations." People who refuse to take a stand, and have an escape or exit strategy for everything, want optimal flexibility. They look for options, exit strategies, and maneuverability so they cannot be held accountable. However, most people produce best when there are clear-cut boundaries, limits, and direction. When managers eliminate wiggle room, people are focused on the defined playing field.

Eliminating wiggle room reduces explaining and rationalizing the lack of performance. Those who waver stay far away from committed language. Their motto is "could have, would have, and should have"—three phrases that excuse and rationalize anything.

"Could Have, Would Have, Should Have"

Speaking That Derails

- "I tried."

- "If only . . ."

- "If not for . . ."

- "I wish I could have . . ."

- "I had hoped . . ."

- "I would have, but . . ."

- "If the circumstances had been different."

Why it doesn't work: The above phrases are used after something has failed, did not work, or when promised results are not delivered. They are used to rationalize and excuse the behavior. Accountability is not expressed, only reasons or excuses.

To eliminate wiggle room, you must hold people accountable for their commitments, promises, and agreements. Without this accountability, things can easily go off-track. When you hear someone using reasons or excuses, challenge them. By removing escape hatches, you hold people accountable not only for performance expectations, but for their own greatness. Powerful leaders demand excellence and get rid of wiggle room by getting down to the business of execution and implementation. Commitments start the process for producing outstanding results—holding people accountable completes it.

Excusing Failure

Speaking That Derails

DIRECT REPORT: "Here are the quarterly results. We didn't do as well as I hoped but then we did have some difficult challenges."

YOU: "Yes, that's unfortunate. We really needed those results. But who could have guessed that we would run into such a competitive situation?"

Why it doesn't work: The direct report is not held accountable. In fact, you affirm his or her reasons. If you believe there are valid reasons for nonperformance, this is acceptable. Of course it's just easier for you to let the person slide rather than confronting the real performance issue, but you have not held the individual accountable.

Holding people accountable raises the bar on performance. It reinforces the leadership message "We will make things happen despite adversity." People should know they will be held accountable in partnership to perform at their highest level.

Holding People Accountable for High Performance
Speaking That Derails

DIRECT REPORT: "Here are the quarterly results. We didn't do as well as I hoped but then we did have some difficult challenges (wiggle room)."

YOU: "I'd like to talk to you about this. You and I spent considerable time defining expectations, and these numbers are far below our target."

DIRECT REPORT: "Well, yeah, but we didn't know what was going to happen with our competitors (more wiggle room)."

YOU: "We rarely know what the competition is going to do. What's different this time?"

DIRECT REPORT: "We had no idea they were going to make such a major market change (trying to solidify wiggle room)."

You: "Two years ago we faced the same challenge. What I am saying to you is that the numbers are not acceptable, even given the competitive situation. I want to discuss what happened and how we can address it on a short-term and long-term basis. I will work side by side with you to turn this situation around."

DIRECT REPORT: (sigh—no wiggle room left)

Why it works: When you are straightforward and refuse to accept excuses and reasons for less-than-acceptable performance, people respond favorably. Holding people accountable is not punitive; it is demanding and rigorous because you must eliminate wiggle room and escape hatches. It is also important to remain committed to the success of people if you want them to walk away with the necessary internal resources to correct the situation.

What happens when people refuse to be nailed down and no matter how hard you try the wiggle room is still there? Refusing to fully commit is a form of resistance. It shows up when a manager is unable to tie the person down to specifics such as the deadline for completion. That's why removing wiggle room is so important. When you are successful in tying a person down to specifics, you have a much better chance for success. When you are unsuccessful, it tells you that there are other issues you must deal with first before you can obtain a full commitment.

-¤-

What People Are Resisting
When They Won't Commit

1. **Commitments in general.** The person does not want to be
   held accountable for commitments, execution, and deliverables. He or she avoids committing to almost everything
   whenever possible or may have a fear of failure or the repercussions from failure. He or she may be more willing to accept
   the consequences for not committing, rather than accepting
   accountability. This is a performance issue in any culture
   where accountability is vital. Forget the commitment and deal
   with the performance issue. Until it is resolved, you will be
   unable to count on the individual fulfilling the commitment
   even if he or she complies.

2. **This commitment in specific.** Something is bothering the
   person about *this* commitment. Maybe it is the project itself
   to which he or she objects. Or perhaps the timing, or other
   people involved, or the demands on travel or time away from
   home. Do not make assumptions about what is bothering the
   individual. Instead, ask, "What specifically about this commitment and/or project concerns you?" If he or she is nonre-
   sponsive you can lead with examples by saying, "Is it the
   deadline for the project, or the fact that you would be reporting to 'X,' or . . . ?" When you list a series of concerns, the
   individual will need to confirm or deny them. By process of
   elimination you will close in on the real issue.

3. **How you are handling the process.** Perhaps you are a little too zealous in tackling wiggle room and the person feels attacked. It may simply take an adjustment in how you are saying something to dissolve the resistance. If altering how you are communicating does not change anything and the individual continues to resist, this often points to a larger relationship issue where he or she feels unsupported, unappreciated, and/or undervalued. When this is the case you will need to stop the discussion under way and refocus on the relationship. Ask, "Have I left you feeling unsupported and unappreciated?"

4. **More stress and pressure in an already overcommitted work-load.** The people asked to do the majority of the work are those who produce results and hence are frequently overcommitted. High achievers will do everything possible to deliver on commitments, including not dealing with their health, family, and other priority personal concerns. Sometimes the most responsible act is to decline a commitment if it compromises your ability to take care of your own well-being. As a leader, be sensitive and look for people who are already overcommitted. Often these are the people you rely on most. Because they are unable to set limits for themselves, you will need to establish boundaries by working with them to ensure they are not overcommitted.

   This type of resistance is subtle. Often the person accepts the commitment and starts showing signs of stress only when you attempt to nail down deadlines. Even then, these good performers may just take a deep breath and plunge in. You must be accountable for making sure the individual does not have too much on his or her plate. The best thing to do when this happens is to withdraw the commitment and revisit it at another time.

There are three kinds of people in the world: those who watch things happen, those who ask what happened, and those who make things happen. These distinctions describe the level at which people participate in life—both in the workplace and at home. The greatest benefits come from the highest level of participation. As a leader, demand and give the highest level.

> **The most fundamental daily choice that must be made is:**
> *Am I going to "wait and see" what happens?*
> *or*
> *Am I going to make things happen?*

Discipline yourself to do three things at all times: (1) Only make commitments and promises you plan to keep, (2) tie down every commitment with a specific time frame, and (3) behave consistently with your words and, when necessary, responsibly break or renegotiate a commitment. Words have tremendous power, but you can throw all of it away in a moment by behaving inconsistently with your commitments. Your words and commitments require discipline to make things happen.

Key Communication Principles

Principle 1: Only make commitments you plan to keep.

Think Twice. Notice how often you make commitments such as "I'll call you tomorrow," or, "I'll send you a copy of this." Do you keep both small and large commitments? You may not think of a remark such as, "I'll call you tomorrow" as a promise, but it is. The question is do you treat all promises and agreements with the same level of rigor and discipline to fulfill them?

Action. Listen for the commitments and promises you make during the next several days. Write them down so you can track them. Observe whether you keep both small and large promises. If 10 people in your life were interviewed about whether you keep your word, how would they respond? Would they say you have a high level of integrity?

Principle 2: Refuse to be seduced by "try" and its friends.

Think Twice. "I'll try," "I'll do my best," and, "I'll take a crack at it" come from the same family of powerless language. These phrases imply an attempt to do something, not a commitment or result. The word *try* and its friends are used in lieu of a real commitment and remove accountability. The fallback position when an effort is ineffective is "I said I'd try and I did. It just didn't work out." Imagine if marriage vows were changed from "I do" to "I'll try." Life would become even more complicated.

Action. Listen to how often you hear the word *try* in your language and when others speak. Count the total number of times the word *try* crops up in one day. If you use "try" more than three times in a day, go to work on replacing it with "I will" or silence. No commitment is better than a false one.

Principle 3: Authentic commitments have time frames and answer the question, "by when."

Think Twice. It is not a real commitment without tying it down in time. "When will this be accomplished," or, "By when will this be completed," are questions that must be answered to make the promise real. You cannot hold people accountable without a full and complete commitment from them.

Action. Ask others to tie down promises and agreements with a specific time. Practice doing this with your commitments. If you notice yourself wiggling on a time frame, you probably are not ready to commit.

9

Holding People Accountable

How to Demand the "Best in Performance" and Get It

Your Purpose

To get the best from yourself and others by **creating a culture of accountability**.

The price of greatness is responsibility.

Winston Churchill

There is a classic story about a pilgrim who discovers that meaning and purpose transform how people view their jobs. This narrative has been told many times, but there is a reason for repetition—to capture the positive lesson over and over again until it becomes an integral part of who we are and how we behave. In the story, the pilgrim is walking through a medieval village in Europe when he comes upon a man at work and asks, "What are you doing?" The man replies without looking up, "I'm chipping stone." The pilgrim walks a little farther and comes upon a second man who is doing the same job and again asks, "What are you doing?" The man looks up briefly at the pilgrim and says, "I'm carving a column." The pilgrim walks farther still and comes upon a third man, doing the same job, and asks, "What is it you are doing?" The third man smiles broadly, throws his arms out and says, "I, sir, am building a cathedral."

Demanding excellence brings out greatness in people and transforms a job into a mission. As the pilgrim story illustrates, it is not what people do that matters; it's how they relate to what they are doing. When people have support, positive coaching, and leaders who hold them accountable for their best, no job or task is too small or insignificant. The ability to learn, grow, and contribute to a shared vision allows people to thrive and excel. Everyone works together toward the singular purpose of building a cathedral.

Instead of chipping stone and just getting the job done, people want to be fired up and inspired. A consistent theme throughout this book is the inner need people have to do their best and for leaders to create the environment and relationships necessary to make this possible. Straight talk and committing with integrity are two critical leadership skills, but there is one more that leads to exceptional leadership—the willingness and ability to hold people accountable. After all, the ultimate measure of success in organizations is effective execution and implementation. Commitments mean nothing unless people are held responsible for deadlines and execution. And straight talk is pointless without demanding and getting results.

When you hear the phrase "holding people accountable," do you think of punitive and corrective action? If you do, you're not alone. Outdated and traditional models reinforce this belief and contribute to the failure of leaders and organizations to effectively hold people accountable. Leaders fear they will damage relationships, lose support, or derail people by demanding accountability. They opt for the safer path of being reasonable, which means less direct and demanding. As a result, the gap between expectations and performance is inconsistently addressed. It's not that leaders lack commitment; they lack a way to hold people accountable without derailing relationships.

Leaders who "walk their talk" and consistently model the behaviors they want from others get the best results. Today, leaders need to leave "reasonable" behind and push beyond perceived limits. They must be unwilling to accept anything less than stellar performance from themselves and others. This chapter focuses on how to build a culture of accountability where people hold each other accountable for the best in performance.

Committed Partnerships Lead to Shorthand Communication

Throughout the book you have learned what it means to be accountable for how your words impact people. What you say and how you say it have a powerful impact on how people perform. Your words make the difference between inspiring and derailing others. Powerful communication skills such as softening a message, disarming anger, and turning complaints into commitments are essential for resolving difficult conversations and providing positive direction. Using these skills on a daily basis produces dramatic improvement in your ability to inspire others and get the results you want.

But there is another bold step for courageous leaders who want to reach for the highest rung on the ladder of success. By understanding and mastering the key communication principles at the end of each chapter, leaders can raise their sights from accountable communication to building a culture of accountability. It's hard to find leaders and organizations that do more than talk about culture. Many aspire and give lip service to this lofty vision, but few do what it takes to instill a climate where people consistently behave as owners, commit with integrity, and produce extraordinary results.

To access performance that goes beyond the ordinary, leaders must engage people at both the intellectual and emotional level. It is not enough to provide strategic business goals and traditional measures of profitability as motivating factors. Capturing the hearts and minds of people requires a higher cause that links an individual's personal sense of purpose to the purpose of the organization. This is true now more than ever. Organizations and leaders can no longer promise job security for life. The business landscape has changed, and leaders must change with it. A new committed partnership must emerge between employees on one hand and leaders and the organization on the other. People will commit when leaders link corporate purpose with a personal sense of purpose by (1) increasing the individual's marketability, value, and worth; (2) creating an environment where people feel inspired to come to work; (3) building a culture of accountability that makes your organization the envy of others and attracts talented people; and (4) contributing to a balanced life that allows work, family, and personal freedom to happily coexist and thrive.

A culture of accountability inspires people at the highest levels by challenging them to transform how they collaborate and work with others to produce unprecedented results. But it doesn't stop there. The daily practice of 100% accountability may start in the workplace, but it weaves into the fabric of people's lives altering who they are and how they behave at the most fundamental level. Their values are reinforced and shaped as they learn to replace casual promises with authentic commitments, talk straight responsibly, and hold themselves and others accountable. People become stronger, more self-confident, and develop the ability to make things happen against all odds.

Isn't this what you want for yourself? Don't you want to have the ability to be powerful and to make a difference in every area of your own life? You can have it all, and so can the people who work for you. A culture of accountability inspires people by providing the behavioral framework for how people are expected to work together. The shift takes place in moving from traditional partnerships to committed partnerships. Agreements are made among people at all levels that allow them to feel safe, supported, and encouraged by one another. In addition to building a culture of accountability, committed partnerships have a shorthand communication all their own. When people know that their leaders and coworkers are committed to their success, they are able to swiftly and accountably deal with issues. Hot buttons are seldom pushed and when they are, people recover quickly. Softening a message is not necessary since people respond best to straight talk. Making false assumptions is replaced with trusting a person's commitment. Speed and flexibility are the hallmarks of committed partnerships. People talk in shorthand communication to cut right to the heart of an issue. Committed partnerships provide the foundation for holding people accountable. Without this, no matter how you say it, the direct nature of holding people responsible is often interpreted as punitive and punishing.

If you choose to build a culture of accountability, you must create committed partnerships with the people who report to you, your peers, and senior management. You cannot do this by mandate. It requires meeting and talking with people to clear up anything from the past that is in the way of a committed partnership. Take accountability for your actions, even if they took place a significant time ago, and commit to a new partnership. The eight essential agreements are powerful promises between two or more people. Use them for your discussions, first as checkpoints to discover what is missing in the partnership, then as promises to each other to create safety and trust.

The Eight Essential Agreements of a Committed Partnership

1. We are committed to the success of each other.

2. We hold one another accountable for the best in performance.

3. We talk straight responsibly.

4. We deliver on our commitments and/or responsibly alter them when necessary.

5. We agree that all information and comments shared are confidential and remain between us.

6. If something is unresolved, we continue the dialogue until there is a mutually acceptable resolution.

7. We recover quickly and learn from our mistakes and break-downs.

8. Strengthening our partnerships is a primary goal in everything we do.

The best way to demand outstanding results and get them is to create a culture of accountability where people can use shorthand communication to swiftly achieve goals. Holding people accountable is a form of shorthand communication. Committed partners expect each other to fulfill promises, keep agreements, and be the best they can be. Everyone acts as an informal leader, raising standards and expectations and demanding full execution from themselves and others. Employees manage up and hold their bosses and senior management accountable for delivering on their commitments. Senior management holds leaders throughout the organization accountable for the same thing. Coworkers collaborate and hold one another accountable for working effectively together. The flow upward, downward, and horizontally reinforces a culture of accountability where everyone speaks up, leads, and holds others accountable.

Committed partnerships give you access to shorthand communication. Holding yourself and others accountable provides the "how to" skills for swift correction and getting the best in performance.

Supporting Senior Management

You are the parent, the role model, and the mentor. It all starts with you. All eyes are watching your every move and listening to every word. When you talk about the importance of collaboration, others watch to see how you engage in partnership. When you speak of accountability, they watch to see if your behavior is consistent with your words. You cannot escape the magnifying glass. When you raise expectations for others, you raise them for yourself.

There are two levels in demanding excellence. Leaders must hold themselves accountable and hold others accountable. The key to effectively managing the gap between commitments and execution is *you*. If you do not model what you expect, you will not produce long-term behavioral change in others. At best your hypocrisy will annoy people when you insist they do things you are unwilling to do.

A critical area in which you are highly visible is how you support senior management. It is easy to fall prey to "we/they" thinking and put senior management, the CEO, or others into the enemy camp. It becomes particularly obvious when major change efforts or new initiatives are introduced. This is where you must hold yourself accountable for collaboration, alignment, and talking straight responsibly. New change efforts that you were not a part of, did not invent, and were not asked to contribute to will test your resolve to walk your talk. How you speak and behave reveals your level of commitment, accountability, and ownership. You cannot create a culture of accountability while building your own empire or withholding your support of companywide initiatives.

People listen carefully to what you do and do not say to assess where you stand with regard to new efforts or changes in the organization. Whether you are a member of the senior leadership team, a mid-level manager, or an informal leader, how you publicly support commitments is critical to your career and leadership advancement.

Let's take a closer look at how your behavior demonstrates your support, or lack of it, of senior management or other parts of the organization. When leaders are not aligned, it shows up in the following behaviors:

- **Silence.** Not talking about the initiative. Silence is a lack of action that sends a strong message of nonsupport.

- **Speaking unfavorably or complaining.** Lack of support and alignment includes unfavorable comments about the initiative and/or people who are heading it up. This includes subtle but deadly remarks such as, "It's not a bad idea, however, . . ." or, "It would have been all right two years ago . . ." Indirect comments attack people and change efforts in a way that send the message, "I don't buy this."

- **Being brief, curt, or abrupt.** People read opposition in the behavior of a manager who avoids or curtails discussion on an important initiative. Being abrupt or cutting others off when they talk about a new program or undertaking sends the message that it is not important to you.

- **Faking it.** This is an attempt to be politically correct and comply with expectations of others. No matter how good you are at acting, people generally know when someone is faking it. They can tell instinctively when someone is not telling the truth. Your career and credibility depend on your authenticity, not your acting ability.

Having a different point of view is normal and expected among hard-charging leaders. However, sitting on the sidelines when you do not agree with an initiative is not acceptable in a culture of accountability. When you are not aligned, action needs to be taken so you can talk to the appropriate person. You do not need to agree with his or her choice, but you must align and support it. You will recall that alignment means setting aside your personal preferences to embrace the agreed-upon action of a larger group of people as if you were the author. It is important to distinguish between agreeing and aligning. Agreeing with someone or something means it matches your personal preferences. It is easy to support an effort when it is your preference. The real conflict comes when you are called upon to support an initiative with which you do not agree. This is where you must determine exactly what is in the way. There are four common roadblocks that get in the way of managers and leaders aligning and supporting a new initiative.

1. **You have insufficient information about purpose, expectations, and accountabilities.** You need a greater understanding of how the new initiative fits into the overall scheme of things. Determine what information you are missing and then talk to the appropriate person(s). Do not wait. If the head of the company or business unit has publicly committed to a major effort, he or she expects your complete support. It is a valid request, however, to obtain additional information so you can be an owner in the process.

Critical Information Questions for New Initiatives

These key questions need to be answered in order to persuade others to support and commit to major change efforts. If you are the person initiating the effort, use these as a guide for communicating. If you are being asked to support an effort, the questions may point to areas of information deficit that need to be addressed.

Company Purpose:

1. How does this initiative support our overall mission?

2. Is this initiative consistent with our strategic objectives?

Initiative Outcomes:

1. What are the "big-picture" outcomes and/or intended results?

2. What are the specific outcomes for various groups (for example, staff group, business unit)?

Priorities with Competing Initiatives:

1. How will this new effort impact other initiatives?

2. What are the priorities?

Accountability for Leading Initiative:

1. Who is accountable for heading up this initiative?

2. Who else is accountable for specific aspects of this initiative?

3. What are the accountabilities of the senior leadership group?

Expectations of Managers and Leaders:

1. What are the expectations of managers leading this effort?

2. Are there different expectations and accountabilities for various levels of leadership?

3. What's in it besides more work for managers and leaders? Why should they be "fired up" about this new effort?

Impact on People:

1. How will this effort impact employees?

2. Will this effort impact some people or groups more than others? If so, how will this be addressed?

Communication:

1. How and when will this initiative be communicated? What is the process? Who is accountable?

2. What role will managers and leaders have in communicating to others?

---

2. **You have insufficient information about the process.** The following process questions are important to people who need details and a more precise understanding of how you get from A to Z. In the launch phase of a new initiative, it is legitimate for many process questions to remain unanswered. However, a specific time period should be established for providing answers. For example, a task force may be assigned to design the implementation process and report back within 30 days after announcing the new effort.

Critical Process Questions for New Initiatives

Implementation and Timing:

1. What is the process for implementation?

2. What are the stages?

3. What is the timing for each stage?

4. What is the estimated time for completion for the entire process?

Benchmarking:

1. What other companies have engaged in a similar effort?

2. What success have they had? What challenges have they encountered? How are we learning from their experiences?

Measuring Results:

1. How will results be measured?

2. What criteria will be established throughout the process to make sure we are on track?

Sustaining Results:

1. How will results be sustained, institutionalized, and integrated with other business practices?

2. How will we effectively transfer from the support of outside consultants to self-sufficiency?

Costs, Expenses, and Budgets:

1. What are the associated costs and expenses?

2. Will these costs come out of individual budgets or a company budget?

3. Will additional resources (for example, people and/or money) be provided?

3. **You think there is a better way.** You are aligned with the desired outcomes and results, but believe there is a better method. Depending on the stage of the process, your input may or may not be useful. If it is early enough to make changes in the process, immediately talk to the appropriate person and provide your input. If you discover it is too late for the type of change you are suggesting or you do not receive a favorable response, just say, "Thank you for listening." There is nothing worse than a manager or leader who presents a recommendation and then acts out when it is rejected.

4. **You strongly disagree with the initiative.** The question that must be answered is "Do you philosophically, morally, and/or ethically disagree with the initiative?" Do you think it violates your values in some way? Think carefully about your response. If your answer is "yes," talk to the appropriate person and express your concern. Often what looks like a conflict in values is a lack of understanding and communication about the positive intentions for a new effort. Your concerns may completely dissolve once you have a better understanding of the commitment and intention behind the initiative.

   On the other hand, if you have talked to the appropriate person(s) and obtained sufficient information, and find there is a conflict of values, you have a decision to make. Values are a deal breaker when it comes to alignment and support. If there is a real conflict between what you believe and what the company is doing, it may be appropriate for you to leave. Faking support and alignment or trying to comply and go along with something that violates your values does not work. It doesn't work for you, and it doesn't work for the company. Others will see right through your façade, and you will be unhappy. This is a last resort and should only be taken if you have exhausted every option to gather information, have a dialogue, and express your concerns.

When you are not fully aligned but still can support the overall objective, have a conversation with the right person. A meaningful dialogue that provides more information will, in all probability, clear up your concerns.

When You Are Not Aligned and *Support* the Outcome
Speaking Accountably

You: "After you announced the new initiative, I had several questions. Is now a good time?"

Your Boss: "Absolutely. What are your questions?"

You: "Before I ask them, I want you to know I support your ideas on building a high-performance organization. We must do this to get to where we want to go."

Your Boss: "That's good to hear. I'm counting on your support."

You: "I know you are and you'll have it. That's why I wanted to speak to you. I want to support you 100 percent on this effort. To do this I need to have a better understanding about . . ."

Why it works: You start with your commitment to the overall objective: building a high-performance organization. This establishes a positive bond of mutual purpose and direction. You both start the conversation knowing you share the same outcome. When you start with concerns or issues, it can lead to a misunderstanding or a debate.

When you have more serious concerns, you may not be able to start by expressing your support of a new initiative. However, you can start by stating your commitment to finding a way to align and support the effort.

When You Are Not Aligned and
Do Not Support the Outcome

Speaking Accountably

You: "After you announced the new initiative, I thought about it and I have concerns that are bothering me."

Your Boss: "Really? What are they?"

You: "Before I address them, I want to explain why I asked to meet with you. I've heard things that, if they are accurate, will keep me from supporting this effort. I'm here because I do not want to operate with assumptions or third-hand information. My outcome is to clear this up so I can fully support you with this effort."

YOUR BOSS: "I'm glad you came to talk with me. I need your support."

YOU: "And I want to give it. Here are my concerns: . . ."

Why it works: You are authentic and straightforward in expressing what is on your mind in an accountable manner. Although you do not start with a commitment to the overall effort, you have started with a commitment to find a way to align and support it. This gives you and your boss a better chance for a positive outcome in what could be a sensitive conversation.

A final message on holding yourself accountable for alignment: Faking it is *not* an option. Managers and leaders are accountable for supporting efforts they personally do not pioneer. If you happen to agree with the initiative, publicly expressing your support is easy. If you do not agree, it is your responsibility to take action and immediately talk with the appropriate person(s). Expressing your concern is necessary to resolve the issue. Alignment does not happen without dialogue. When you make the need to align a personal mission, you can find a way to align with almost every new effort. You just have to be willing to work at it.

Holding yourself accountable is essential. If you demand 100% accountability, collaboration, and responsible straight talk from others, you need to practice it with everyone and in all circumstances. You cannot alter the behavior of others without doing this. The most difficult part of creating a culture of accountability is not inspiring people, it is the requirement that leaders master what they ask of others. People pay attention to the consistency between your words and behavior. Leave a gap, and they will treat your behavior as the real message and throw out your words. People will do as you do.

Managing Up

In a culture of accountability, leaders give subordinates permission to manage up and coach. In traditional organizational models, coaching is a top-down practice where managers provide feedback, input, and correction to those who report to them. Managing up is the reverse process where confident and secure leaders create an open and safe environment for people to speak up. People are encouraged to coach their boss and others senior to them by providing responsible straight talk, requests for action, and specific feedback on what is needed from him or her as a leader. Coaching and holding others accountable is viewed as everyone's job and is not limited to leaders. When leaders allow others to contribute to them by coaching, it sends a positive message to the organization. Others feel they can speak up without fear of repercussions. People respond well to the open, supportive, and encouraging environment that is created.

Managing up is an alien concept that organizations claim they promote but in reality does not exist. Employees do not believe that leaders want straightforward input and feedback. They have learned to be politically correct and say what leaders want to hear. If you are sincere about creating a culture of accountability, you must give people explicit permission to coach you each time you talk. Although it may sound repetitious and unnecessary to you, people need to hear you say the words that give them freedom to contribute. What would happen if you said, "I love you," to your spouse the day you got married, but never said it again? Would this be a problem? Just because you said it once does not mean you do not need to say it again.

Invite People to Manage Up and Coach You
Speaking Accountably

- "What coaching do you have for me? What can I do better? I need your feedback."

- "What advice do you have for me?"

- "What would you do in my position?"

- "Am I off base? What have I missed?"

- "What are the flaws in my thinking? Help me with this."

- "I don't have all the answers. I need your help on thinking this through."

- "How can I provide you with better support? I'd like your coaching."

- "Please give me your view about how I am doing on leading our group/organization. Do I inspire or derail people? What do I need to do differently?"

Why it works: When you actively seek coaching, people feel acknowledged that you want their input. There are two things to remember: (1) Give people permission to coach you frequently by asking for their input, and (2) when you receive coaching, listen carefully and thank them whether you agree or not.

Permission statements are direct statements requesting feedback. Do not assume the absence of input means people do not have feedback, coaching, or opinions. It only means they do not feel safe in expressing them. Invite others to provide their input and when they do, listen carefully and always thank them. Sometimes you are moving so fast that people think you don't have time to listen. At other times you may appear to be decided or closed on an issue and people feel their input is useless. Be accountable for your impact.

Inviting others to coach you is one thing, but how good are you at managing up to your boss? Do you have a committed partnership where you can safely and openly hold each other accountable? Do you coach others senior to you? If you don't, what's missing in the relationship that prevents you from managing up? Be courageous and have a conversation with the individual about what you need and want from the partnership. Nothing happens unless you make it happen. Relationships take work, and business partnerships are no exception.

The easiest way to manage up is to (1) first ask for permission to provide feedback and coaching and (2) align with the individual's commitment before you coach or make a request.

⌈◇⌉

When Your Request to Manage Up Is Declined

Speaking Accountably

YOU: "At our last staff meeting I had a couple of observations I want to share with you. I see a way you can eliminate a lot of resistance to our new initiative and make sure it gets successfully off the ground. Do you want this input?"

YOUR BOSS: "Yes, I do. I'm sick and tired of people resisting. But right now I want to talk about the problem we're having with . . ."

Why it works: You started with something that is of major importance to your boss—eliminating resistance to the new initiative. Even though he or she is not ready to talk about this now, you have piqued his or her interest. Move to the next step and hold him or her accountable for a specific time when you can provide coaching and feedback.

Don't let your boss off the hook. There must be a reason behind the resistance. Try again to hold him or her accountable.

⫸⫷

Getting Permission to Manage Up and Coach

Speaking Accountably

YOU: "We do need to handle this current situation fast. When is a good time to have the conversation about what you can do to eliminate resistance?"

YOUR BOSS: "Sometime this week."

YOU: "How about tomorrow? I'll set up the meeting."

YOUR BOSS: "Good, tomorrow will work. Now, let's take a look at . . ."

Why it works: Managing up and holding those above you accountable takes perseverance in obtaining permission and finding the right time to coach. What constitutes the "right time" is when your boss or others are not preoccupied and can really listen to what you have to say. By reinforcing what your boss wants and speaking directly to his or her commitment, which is to successfully launch a new initiative, you contribute instead of complain or criticize.

You display your strength of character as a leader when you are tenacious and rigorous in going after what you want, especially when it comes to dealing with people above you. Most senior executives and leaders will tell you they prefer strong managers and leaders who are willing to talk straight and challenge them. Sure, these same executives and leaders may react or go toe to toe with you, but this doesn't mean they don't want to be challenged. It may only reveal their preferred method for processing information, which is to debate out loud. Many executives have the need to verbally spar in order to gain access to a new way of thinking.

If you tend to avoid conflict and prefer harmonious discussions to intense debates, you may need to broaden your comfort level and skill base. By the time someone reaches the senior executive level, they know how to engage in rigorous debate. Even if this is not their preferred mode of communication, developing this skill has been necessary for survival among others who use it. Verbal sparring allows many people to access new ways of thinking, to push and be pushed back. When you challenge others in a positive way, you help them think in different categories. The most important thing to remember is that you have something to contribute; you are not there to criticize or complain. You are there to manage up and add value to your boss or others senior to you. It is up to you to make sure your contribution is heard.

⊷⊶

Creating a Positive Framework to Manage Up

Speaking Accountably

You: "Thanks for making time to see me. As I mentioned before, I had some observations from our last staff meeting about how you can eliminate resistance to our new initiative. Are you open to my input now?"

Your Boss: "Yes, I am. I'd like to hear your thoughts. I'm about ready to dump a bunch of people and hire others who will get with the program."

Why it works: You restated the commitment your boss has to the new initiative. A positive framework has been established so he is open to hearing what you have to say.

In the sample dialogue, the leader's boss is not ready to take accountability for his impact. Instead he is pointing the finger at others. Your job, as the leader, is to ensure that he takes accountability for his impact so that the real issue can be resolved. Let him know that he has power over his own behavior. He can't keep hiring new people, but he can take a look at how his power is impacting others.

Managing Up and Holding Others Accountable for Their Impact

Speaking Accountably

YOU: "I would not be so fast to conclude that the difficulty is with the managers. I believe they are committed to the new initiative."

YOUR BOSS: "Committed? How can they be committed and do nothing?"

YOU: "They are doing a lot. In fact, they are doing everything they can with the direction they have."

YOUR BOSS: "Are you saying they need more direction? How many times do I have to repeat myself and say the same thing over and over?"

YOU: "I know you are frustrated. But the answer is not changing the members of your senior group. The key is for you to create a cohesive team. Would you like to hear what I think you can do to turn things around and get people on board?"

YOUR BOSS: "Yes, of course, I want to get people on board. I'm just frustrated. Tell me your thoughts."

YOU: "People do not feel safe to speak up and tell you what is on their minds. Let's find a way to help them feel comfortable with you."

Why it works: You have stayed right with the conversation and not once have you deferred, waffled, or agreed with your boss in order to get "out of the heat." Your boss is reacting and going toe to toe with you. So what? Stay with the discussion and bring your boss back to his or her commitment. No matter what people react to, their commitment remains unwavering. When you return to it, a solid foundation and base are provided as the backdrop for the conversation.

Managing up is often uncomfortable, especially when you are in the beginning stages of establishing a committed partnership. If you can't manage up to your boss and others, your subordinates may question your accountability. They will wonder why you expect them to take risks and manage up to you when you are unwilling to do the same. Model courageous and accountable leadership by being all you can be as a leader. Trust yourself; push the envelope, and forge committed partnerships with those above you. Actively coach and manage up so you are viewed as a positive contributor and a strong leader who is willing to speak up.

Circles of Trust

Now we're getting down to the crux of the matter. It all comes down to trust. You must trust yourself enough to take risks and hold others accountable. And you must trust others enough to get behind them 100 percent and help them get back on track when they falter. Trust is the basis for committed partnerships. You're not perfect and neither are they, but the quality of relationship that exists in a committed partnership allows people to take risks because they know they are not alone. In Chapter 8 we discussed how to express your commitment to a person's success. Here we delve deeper to examine how to trust others.

Let's start with some basic questions: Do you trust that people have an inner need to grow, learn, and contribute? Do you trust people to do their best, or do people have to demonstrate results before you believe in them? These are fundamental questions you must answer to discover how you inspire or derail people.

Think of trust as a series of concentric circles with the centermost circle—the bull's-eye—being your inner circle of trust. Do people start on the outside and have to earn your trust to get to the inner circle? Or do you trust people and place them within your inner circle without their having to earn a place? Many parents place their children within the inner circle of trust without proof, validation, or the need to meet specific criteria. They unconditionally believe in their children and want them to succeed. Placing children in the center circle of trust is not difficult.

In organizations, many leaders make people earn their place before they trust them. This creates a catch-22. When people must earn your support to become part of your inner circle, they lack the very thing they need to excel—your belief in them. This creates a built-in failure mechanism. People must prove themselves to you. Now they have two battles to fight instead of one—handling daily business challenges and earning your approval. Admittedly, there are some people who will rise to the challenge of proving their worth and value. They thrive on overachieving and disproving lackluster beliefs of others. However, the majority of people need a leader who unconditionally believes in them. When you support people from the beginning before they have earned your trust, success is much more probable.

We can reduce this idea to two simple categories of leadership expectations: (1) *"Earn my trust"* or (2) *"You have my trust."* There is a world of difference between these two approaches. "Earn my trust" sends a message that a person must win your approval. When a leader has an earn-my-trust expectancy, it shows up in words and behavior. Often the words sound positive but carry a subtle, conditional "if" message, which questions if the person can really rise to your expectations.

"Earn My Trust" Message
Speaking That Derails

Message: "I'd like you to take on this assignment. See if you can get people on board. I doubt whether you can get everyone, but give it a shot."

Why it doesn't work: It sounds positive, but this statement carries a subtle message that communicates, "I don't think you can do this." The language is tentative such as, "See if you can . . ." and "I doubt whether you can . . ." The leader is either resigned about the assignment and/or has a lack of belief in what the individual is capable of doing. There is no leadership expression of support or belief in the person.

In Chapter 3, we talked about people giving *you* the gift of trust. The opposite is also true—you must give others the gift of trust if you want people to perform at the highest levels possible. You can set people up to succeed or fail. They will fulfill your expectations either way. Communicate positive expectations by sending you-have-my-trust messages. People do not want to disappoint you. They want you to be proud of their efforts, and they want to be acknowledged as a significant contributor in the larger mission.

"You Have My Trust" Message

Speaking Accountably

Message: "This assignment is perfect for you. Use your ability to enroll people and get everyone on board. They won't be able to resist your persuasiveness. I know you can do this."

Why it works: The manager clearly reinforces the ability of the individual to succeed in the assignment. If the individual doubts his or her own capability, the confidence and belief of the leader will help him or her over this hurdle. Positive expectations and "you have my trust" messages from leaders can move a person from mediocre to outstanding performance.

When you believe in someone and you verbally articulate it, that person's confidence and ability to perform soar. It also lets you provide input, feedback, and coaching. People will hear your coaching as positive when they know you trust them. When you make others earn your trust, a small percentage of the population will rise to the occasion and succeed. The majority will not. They will feel as if you are waiting for them to fail, ready to pounce at the slightest indiscretion. People who prefer working in organizations rather than working on their own want an environment of support, trust, and belonging. Your behavior and words set the tone and establish the climate in which people will succeed or fail. It is the responsibility of leaders to create a positive climate and give people the gift of trust to ensure they succeed.

Five Steps for Holding Others Accountable

When you coach others, make sure you have their permission. You may want to start a coaching conversation by saying, "Are you open to feedback?" If they're not, you need to work on the relationship. If they are, this gives them time to adjust to how to listen to the conversation.

Remember to listen for the unspoken answer when you ask for permission to coach. Your question, "Are you open to feedback?" may elicit a response such as, "Well, I guess so. What did I do wrong?" The answer may sound like a "yes," but this person may not be ready for positive coaching, or may need more reassurance first. When this happens, do not provide coaching at the moment. Talk about your partnership. It may be helpful to review the eight agreements of a committed partnership to find out what is missing. To make it safe for the person to speak up, you will need to take accountability. You could say, "I must not be doing a good job in letting you know how much I support you. There is obviously something I am not doing or saying that is important to you. What's on your mind?" Reestablish your committed partnership, then again ask for permission to coach. Without a positive response, people are not ready to hear your feedback and coaching and you will waste your time and theirs.

To develop people and help them grow, you must unleash untapped capabilities and build their confidence. This type of development requires holding people accountable for what is possible and for their commitments. Leaders must rigorously manage the gap between promises and execution.

When you are disappointed, do you tend to blow up or clam up? These are the two most common responses of leaders when breakdowns occur. Neither produces positive action. The five-step model provides a clear, step-by-step process for handling problems, breakdowns, or specific performance issues. This is a model for shorthand communication. It starts with the assumption that you have a committed partnership and you can talk straight responsibly without preamble or qualifiers. The model is a direct, no-nonsense approach to handling a breakdown and recovering quickly. Implicit is the commitment to the success of each other.

The five-step model can be used for broken promises and agreements, missed deadlines, unacceptable performance, and miscommunication for demanding the best from people. The model establishes a partnership conversation with the emphasis on correcting the situation, preventing it from recurring, and strengthening the relationship.

The Five-Step Model for Holding People Accountable

Step 1: Declare the Breakdown

- What is the problem: miscommunication or breakdown?

Step 2: Accept Accountability

- How did your behavior contribute to the breakdown?

- What did you do, or not do, that impacted the situation?

- How did the behavior of others contribute to the breakdown?

Step 3: Align on Immediate Corrections

- What needs to be done immediately?

- Who is accountable for making this happen?

- What other people need to be included and/or advised?

- How fast can this happen? What is the due date?

Step 4: Align on Long-Term Corrections

- What preventive measures need to be put in place?

- Who is accountable for making this happen?

- What other people need to be included and/or advised?

- By when will this happen?

Step 5: Build the Relationship

- What have we learned?

- What are we going to do differently?

- What positive impact will this have on our relationship?

Declaring the breakdown is the first step in the model. Unless you identify specifically what needs to be addressed, it is not possible to hold people accountable. Getting agreement on the breakdown can be challenging. Unless both parties agree that "X" is the problem, there is nothing to which you can hold people accountable. Following is a sample conversation using Step 1: Declare the Breakdown.

> YOU: "I think we have a miscommunication. I expected to receive your proposal yesterday."

> SUBORDINATE: "I am so far behind. I'm still working on it."

> YOU: "I know you have a great deal to do. Missing your deadline and not communicating affects not only me but also many others."

> SUBORDINATE: "Yeah, well, I'll get it done as soon as I can. "

> YOU: "I need to know that you understand how missing this deadline has impacted others."

> SUBORDINATE: "I didn't realize they were waiting for my input."

> YOU: "How can they proceed without it? You have information they need to make important decisions."

> SUBORDINATE: "I didn't think about that. I was so focused on everything else."

> YOU: "Thanks for being honest. I think this is where everything went off-track. You were focused on what you needed to do instead of working collaboratively and making this a team effort."

> SUBORDINATE: "That's accurate. I felt I was alone in this and completely forgot about partnering with others."

While declaring the breakdown, the crucial outcome is to make sure the individual understands how his or her behavior impacts others. Be sure the person is accountable for that impact. Obtain agreement on the nature of the problem or breakdown before moving on to the next step.

The second step in the model is to accept accountability for your impact. Sometimes it may feel as if you have no accountability for what happened. This is seldom, if ever, true. If you are a leader, you are accountable for everything that occurs with subordinates. In some way you have contributed to the breakdown or problem. By accepting accountability you are not accepting blame; instead you are strengthening the relationship. For example, see the conversation below to find out how to build the relationship by accepting accountability for your impact.

> SUBORDINATE (continued from step 1): "That's accurate. I felt I was alone in this and completely forgot about partnering with others."

> YOU: "I can see where I dropped the ball. I needed to talk with you about the entire process so you had the big picture of what is happening."

> SUBORDINATE: "Well, you did tell me some things."

> YOU: "But not enough. It's my responsibility to make sure you have clear expectations from me. I expected you to understand how others would use your proposal, but I never told you this."

> SUBORDINATE: "Well, I could have asked you to explain the process to me. That's my responsibility to understand why I'm doing something and to make sure it's on target."

When a leader accepts accountability for how he or she has contributed to the situation, it opens up the conversation. Although you should never expect it, once you express your accountability it is not uncommon for others to express theirs. A leader's statement of accountability shows ownership and makes it a shared problem that will be worked through together.

After you have accepted accountability for your impact, move on to step 3. Many problems need attention fast. The continuing conversation below demonstrates how to align on immediate corrections so people can go into action to control the damage and impact on others.

> SUBORDINATE (continued from step 2): "Well, I could have asked you to explain the process to me. That's my responsibility to understand why I'm doing something and to make sure it's on target."

> YOU: "We both learned something from this. Let's decide on what we need to do to minimize the impact on others."

> SUBORDINATE: "I need to communicate and apologize for being late with the proposal. I will let everyone know that they will have the proposal in their hands by Wednesday morning."

> YOU: "That's great. When are you going to communicate and who will be included?"

> SUBORDINATE: "I'll send an e-mail as soon as I walk out of here. I'll include the six people on the task force, plus I'll copy you along with the head of Claims."

It's specific. All elements for an immediate correction have been covered in the above conversation. The subordinate has taken accountability to act and the action is clear. The new deadline has been established along with the timing of the communication to others apologizing for the delay. Finally, those who need to know what happened will be included.

There may be times when you need to break the conversation into two parts. First, have a discussion that includes steps 1 through 3 and ends with alignment on immediate short-term corrections. This allows you to deal with urgent situations. Later, you can come back to the discussion after the problem has been handled and have a conversation that covers steps 4 and 5. The final two steps are important, so make sure you cover them. They support continuous learning and strengthening of the relationship. Following the same conversation as above, we now move to step 4—Align on Long-Term Corrections—and continue the process.

> SUBORDINATE (continued from step 3): "I'll send an e-mail as soon as I walk out of here. I'll include the six people on the task force, plus I'll copy you along with the head of Claims."
>
> YOU: "Sounds good. Let's talk about what we need to do to avoid future breakdowns. I'll start with what I can do. I will spend time up front with you on what others are doing and how all the pieces will come together."
>
> SUBORDINATE: "That would help. And I'll stay in touch with you throughout the project to make sure things are on track. I will also make sure I make my deadlines."

The preventive actions in the conversation above are between the two people involved and do not require including others. This is not a complicated problem to solve. It requires recommitting to being accountable for working together to produce the desired results.

Finally, a culture of accountability is based on recovery and learning. Mistakes, miscommunication, and problems are opportunities to learn and build the relationship. Discussing what is learned from breakdowns and challenges needs to become a leadership habit. It is all too easy with a hectic schedule to ignore the relationship and what has been learned and move on to solve the next problem. In the final section of the conversation, the leader and subordinate can now begin to use step 5—Build the Relationship—now that the issue has been resolved.

> SUBORDINATE (continued from step 4): "That would help. And I'll stay in touch with you throughout the project to make sure things are on track. I will also make sure I make my deadlines."

> YOU: "I appreciate your commitment. I think we've both learned something from this. I've learned that I need to be a better communicator and work closer with you throughout the process."

> SUBORDINATE: "This was a wake-up call for me. I need to be much more aware of my impact on others before, during, and at the end of a project."

> YOU: "Is there anything else we should discuss? How has this discussion impacted you?"

> SUBORDINATE: "Well, it's been positive. I came in here feeling defensive but now I feel that we've worked this out together."

New promises have been made so that people can count on one another. At the end of step 5, the question is asked, "How has this discussion impacted you?" This provides an opportunity for both parties to see if there is anything else to be said and make sure the conversation ends in partnership and moving forward in a positive direction.

Holding people accountable is a positive leadership action. It makes people responsible for doing their best and behaving consistently with their commitments. The five-step model allows you to handle problems without pointing the finger. Most importantly, people know they are being held to high standards by a leader who is committed to their success.

Building a Culture of Accountability

Building ownership in others is a journey, not an event. It is an ongoing process emphasizing quick recovery and learning from mistakes and breakdowns. When people understand that 100% accountability is a way of life, they begin to see the endless possibilities. This cannot be a "program of the month" in anyone's eyes. The practices of accountability need to be integrated throughout your business. People need to see it in you, and see that it is expected of them. Building a culture of accountability is a process worth undertaking, a process that makes your life and the lives around you much easier. It creates smooth day-to-day business operations and removes the complicated, time-consuming issues involved in miscommunication and misunderstandings.

To build a culture of accountability, leaders must learn how to speak a new language. In the traditional 50/50 culture where finger-pointing, blame, and "I'll do my part" thinking dominates, the language lacks inspiration. In a 50/50 culture a leader may say, "We need to deal with this change and how it has impacted our business." Listen to the difference when the leader says, "We will embrace this change and use it as an opportunity to move our business into a new market." The first statement reports change while the second statement describes what is possible.

It takes a different language to speak a new future into existence and build a culture of accountability. When leaders deal with mistakes, problems, and breakdowns in a 50/50 culture they might say, "This should never have happened. You need to handle it fast." In this statement there is a harsh judgment and reprimand. The use of the word *you* underscores that the person who made the mistake is alone in correcting it. In a culture of accountability leaders would say, "We made a mistake. The question is, How are we going to recover quickly and learn from this?" By the use of inclusive language and using the word we, the leader acknowledges the mistake and moves the focus to recovering quickly and capturing what can be learned.

In a culture of accountability, people are held responsible for their impact on results and others. For example, in a 50/50 environment, leaders might say, "What you did is all right, but see if you can do better." The use of incremental language such as "better" demands little in the way of improved performance nor does it express much belief in the person. In a climate of 100% accountability, leaders use shorthand communication with committed partners and say, "What you delivered is not acceptable for what you can do. I know what you are capable of producing and I won't accept anything less. Now let's work together to . . ." Talking straight responsibly and demanding outstanding performance is a trademark of leaders who build a culture of accountability. Mediocre, ordinary, or average performance is not acceptable for the leader or for anyone else. Leaders challenge people to stretch and reach higher, not in incremental steps but by taking a leap of faith and making the impossible happen.

By using the language and phrases in the 100% Accountability column, you can begin the process of helping people think in different ways. Building new habits and behaviors requires a new language or that new meaning be given to old language. Our words and phrases lead people down a particular path. Do you want people to try and do something or do you want them to do it? Your language and words will directly influence what they do.

The new language of 100% accountability is inspirational. It demands more of what people want to give—their discretionary effort for a higher purpose. Give people a reason beyond profitability that supports their personal purpose and they will embrace change, act as owners, and make things happen. A culture of accountability is a higher purpose. It is a journey and a mission. It asks people to develop, learn, and grow. It impacts their personal and professional lives. And it connects and bonds people in a way that few experience. People learn about the power of working together in committed partnerships. In all of this, people find a higher cause they can embrace as both a personal and organizational mission.

AVOID	REPLACE WITH
50/50 Accountability	100% Accountability
• Do your share; do your part.	• Accept accountability, not blame.
• See what you can do.	• Work together, collaborate, partner, work as a team.

- Deal with change; handle change.
- Be politically correct.
- Don't make mistakes.
- Don't make the mistake again.
- Agree or comply with others.
- Tolerate what you don't like.
- Complain and criticize.
- Try to make things happen.
- Commit casually.
- Have ordinary partnerships.
- Put up with senior management.
- Earn trust.
- Ignore the past.
- Produce good results.

- Embrace change; use change as an opportunity.
- Talk straight responsibly.
- Recover quickly.
- Learn from mistakes.
- Align and support others.
- Be an owner.
- Make requests to move the action forward.
- Make things happen.
- Commit with integrity.
- Build committed partnerships.
- Manage up to senior management.
- Give the gift of trust.
- Clean up the past.
- Produce extraordinary results.

- Do your job and let others do theirs.
- Hold yourself and others accountable.

Building a culture of accountability takes commitment and drive. It takes strong leaders who are willing to make bold commitments in the face of challenging circumstances. A leader must commit to being 100% accountable for his or her impact on results and people. It's a big commitment, but the results can be staggering. Single-handedly, you can transform the attitude of the people in your organization from victims to owners, where people move off the sidelines and into the game. You can replace blame and finger-pointing with responsible action and collaboration. You can quit refereeing conflicts between people. You can create a culture of accountability where people feel safe to speak up and contribute. And you can dramatically and positively alter the lives of people as they grow and develop in ways they never thought possible. All of this you can do if you are willing to hold yourself accountable as the role model and mentor for others. Take yourself on as a project. Invite others to manage up and coach you. Stretch yourself and engage in learning "what you don't know you don't know." Change your behavior, and others will change theirs. You do not need to wait for anything or anyone. It is within your power to make change happen.

In the story at the beginning of this chapter, the pilgrim who walked through the village asked three people what they were doing. Each person described the same job differently from chipping stone to building a cathedral. In a culture of accountability, people reach for the sky and build cathedrals. This transformation occurs when people feel energized and inspired by a leader who believes in them and demands the best from them.

Winston Churchill said it best: "History will be kind to me for I intend to write it." This is the choice you must make in deciding to embark on the journey of 100% accountability. You can be an owner and write history or you can allow history to be written. It's up to you. Decide now to inspire others by learning to say it right the first time, and to recover quickly when you don't.

Only you can decide what type of leader you want to be and the legacy you want to create. This much is true—you can do and accomplish far more than you ever thought possible by demanding the best in performance first from yourself and then from others. Holding people accountable is the linchpin for high performance, and you are the key to making it happen in your organization. Don't wait for others. Start today and write history.

Key Communication Principles

Principle 1: Hold yourself and others accountable for the best in performance.

Think Twice. People prefer leaders who are demanding in the name of excellence and quality. What you demand from others you must be willing to demand of yourself. As you raise the bar on holding people accountable, discover where you can demand more from yourself.

Action. Eliminate reasons, excuses, and justifications from your speaking. When you notice yourself defending or justifying, stop and take accountability.

Principle 2: Walk your talk. When you don't, people will believe your behaviors and discount your words.

Think Twice. What you want from others you must do yourself. It's as simple as that. You are the role model and others follow your lead. If you want others to respond favorably to your coaching and input, then respond positively to theirs. There are no special privileges as a leader. You cannot opt out of being accountable for doing what you ask of others.

Action. Focus on actively seeking personal coaching from others. Ask, "How can I be a better leader/boss/partner for you?" When people respond, listen carefully and thank them for their contributions.

Principle 3: Building a culture of accountability is a journey, not an event.

Think Twice. Accountability is not a skill; it is a mindset. How people relate to circumstances and one another reveals their level of accountability. Coaching and holding people accountable are two significant elements of an accountable culture. The most important message you can send is that building a culture of accountability is not a program of the month; it is a journey and a way of doing business.

Action. Share with others what you have learned about being an owner and accepting accountability. Ask others to tell you what they have discovered about themselves.

Principle 4: Supporting something you did not invent is a test of your strength of character.

Think Twice. It is easy to support people and initiatives with which you agree. The difficulty is when you need to align with major efforts you would not have chosen. But the point is, it wasn't your decision. There are times when you get to vote, and there are times when your vote is not requested. During these times it is your job to find a way to authentically align and support others both publicly and privately.

Action. Take a look at how you are publicly demonstrating your support for senior management, major initiatives, and change efforts. If something is missing in your ability to support someone or something, take immediate action and talk to the appropriate person. Nothing happens without communication.

Index

About the Author

Dr. Malandro and her team of experts work with organizations to build personal accountability, communication, and leadership skills that result in *people working together to produce unprecedented results.* The Malandro technology, a highly structured and proven process, quickly mobilizes people to proactively lead change, collaborate, and improve earnings through increased efficiency and effectiveness. Loretta Malandro, Ph.D., is president and CEO of Malandro Communication Inc., an organization with over 20 years' experience working with 5000 corporations worldwide. Executives whose mission is to lead a *great* company, not just a good one, engage Malandro for rapid, sustainable results.

Loretta Malandro and her organization can be reached by:

E-mail: partners@malandro.com
Telephone: 480-970-3200
Facsimile: 480-970-0205

Web site: www.malandro.com

Malandro Communication Inc.
Scottsdale, AZ 85250
U.S.A.